Herding Cats

Herding Cats

A Strategic Approach to Social Media Marketing

Andrew Rohm and Michael Weiss

businessexpert
Press

Herding Cats: A Strategic Approach to Social Media Marketing
Copyright © Business Expert Press, LLC, 2014.

First published in 2014 by
Business Expert Press, LLC
222 East 46th Street, New York, NY 10017
www.businessexpertpress.com

ISBN-13: 978-1-60649-838-5 (paperback)
ISBN-13: 978-1-60649-839-2 (e-book)

Business Expert Press Digital and Social Media Marketing and Advertising Collection

Collection ISSN: 2333-8822 (print)
Collection ISSN: 2333-8830 (electronic)

Cover and interior design by Exeter Premedia Services Private Ltd., Chennai, India

First edition: 2014

10 9 8 7 6 5 4 3 2 1

Printed in the United States of America.

Abstract

One of the top marketing challenges that marketing managers and executives face today is to better understand social media and its promise as a marketing platform. The social media ecosystem, including traditional platforms such as Facebook and Twitter and upstarts such as Instagram and Snapchat, have evolved significantly over the past 10 years, so much so that keeping pace with the latest social media platforms can seem like herding cats. To help you craft a more strategic approach to your social media efforts, we provide a timeless perspective on how to create, manage, and measure social media content. We simplify the concept of branding and advertising fueled by social media to one that focuses on understanding your *why* (Chapter 1); fostering customer engagement (Chapter 2) through crafting your organization's unique story (Chapter 3); telling the story strategically via social media channels (Chapter 4); organizing for social media and managing, monitoring, and measuring your social media efforts as well as developing guidelines and governance policies for executing your social media strategy (Chapter 5); identifying key metrics and measuring performance through analytics (Chapter 6); learning from several social media best practice examples (Chapter 7); and understanding the extent of change brought on by digital and social media related to how you engage your customers (Chapter 8).

This book is intended to provide the reader—whether an upper level undergraduate or MBA student, social media manager, brand manager, small business owner, corporate executive, or simply someone who wishes to better understand the intersection of business and social media—important perspectives and frameworks on developing and managing an effective social media strategy.

Keywords

advertising, analytics, branding, brand storytelling, customer engagement, customer relationship management, digital marketing, metrics, social media marketing

Contents

Preface

According to a recent poll of marketing executives and academics, one of the top marketing challenges for 2014 included the ability to better understand social media and execute social media campaigns. Indeed, keeping track of the latest social media platforms can seem like herding cats (to be honest, we've never herded a cat; yet we can imagine the challenges involved in such a process). This is because the social media ecosystem has evolved significantly over the past 10 years. In 2004, it was Facebook. Twitter came along in 2006. In 2010, it was Instagram and Pinterest, with Snapchat and Vine following close behind in 2011 and 2012, respectively. As we write this, Instagram's new video-sharing feature and Facebook's Paper platform will soon seem, like, so 2013 and 2014.

Even the best-selling books on social media, books that propose to have the winning strategy of tomorrow, confess that the strategies of today are different than they were five years ago. Just like (we imagine) the process of herding cats, the risk is that we simply cannot keep up with the rapid changes that take place in the new world of marketing and advertising.

In this book, we don't promise to offer the latest, yet soon outdated, tactics for developing and executing a social media campaign. What we seek to do, however, is provide a timeless perspective on how to create, manage, and measure social media content—a perspective that is relevant and applicable to companies, organizations, and brands, large, small, and medium sized. In addition, in chapters one through six, we've developed several *action step* sections that are designed to spur you and your team, your group, department, or organization to take steps—action steps—toward crafting a better, more strategic, approach to your social media efforts.

Yogi Berra, the New York Yankee catcher, once observed, "If you don't know where you are going, you might wind up someplace else." He also remarked, "The future ain't what it used to be." Both of these statements ring true today as C-suite executives, marketing and advertising directors, brand managers, and you (the reader of this book) struggle to understand the role of social media within the organization. The social media landscape is a complex space—populated by (now) traditional platforms such as Facebook, Twitter, Google+, and LinkedIn as well as new entrants to the party such as Instagram, Pinterest, Vine, Snapchat, and even the revived MySpace.

The social media landscape can be confusing, especially to those of us who were born, raised, and socialized prior to the emergence of the Internet back in the mid-1990s. Let us state now that we believe *simple* is good. We also believe that the world of marketing and branding has become needlessly complex and complicated, due, in part, to rapid shifts and advances in technology and due, in part, to business books that seek to overcomplicate (definition: the opposite of simplify) the content contained in competing texts and books.

By contrast, this book aims to simplify the concept of branding and advertising fueled by social media to one that focuses on understanding your *why* (Chapter 1); fostering customer engagement (Chapter 2) through crafting your organization's unique story (Chapter 3); telling the story strategically via social media channels (Chapter 4); organizing for social media and managing, monitoring, and measuring your social media efforts, as well developing guidelines and governance policies for executing your social media strategy (Chapter 5); identifying key metrics and measuring results through analytics (Chapter 6); learning from several social media best practice examples (Chapter 7); and understanding the extent of change brought on by digital and social media in relation to how you build and maintain intimate relationships with your customers (Chapter 8).

So, back to Yogi, if you and your company or organization (large, small, or medium sized) don't understand or aren't able to communicate where you want to go in terms of your ultimate internal organizational and customer-facing objectives, it will also be difficult to effectively harness social media to help you achieve those objectives. The challenge is that today's technology, in the form of the new and improved tablet, mobile device or application, and revolutionary new social media platform, risks ending up at the bottom of the birdcage tomorrow.

Your customers are changing too. They're no longer passive participants in the company–customer relationship. They expect a lot from you—they want timely information (now, not tomorrow!), they demand a role in helping tell your organization's or brand's story as well as wanting a hand in helping you develop your own products or services, and conversely, they are more than willing to trash your company to friends and peers and anyone else who will listen (or read) if things don't go their way. In short, they're spoiled rotten and want you to feed them grapes—and who can blame them!

That's why we felt a book such as this is so important today. We also need to emphasize what this book is not: It is *not* a how-to book containing the 10 rules or the 3 magic steps to crafting a successful social media strategy, complete with soon-to-be-outdated examples of platforms and company examples that have little or no application to your unique situations. What this book represents, however, is a guide to thinking strategically and timelessly about the role and use of social media within your organization.

Social Media from 30,000 Feet

It's amazing, really, how fast online social media platforms such as Facebook, Instagram, Pinterest, LinkedIn, and Twitter have grown and how influential they've become. Facebook began in 2004 as a site for Harvard undergrads to meet and, dare we say, hook up. If Facebook were a country, it would today be the world's third largest, with over one billion registered users. Perhaps because of its scope and reach, research even suggests that one in every five divorces today is attributed to Facebook. This fact underlines the influence that the Facebook platform has on us as social beings.

LinkedIn was launched in 2003 as a social networking site for business professionals and recently surpassed 225 million registered users. Twitter was launched in 2006 as a social platform characterized by its tweets of 140 or fewer characters, and has since grown to over 500 million users around the globe. And, of course there are numerous other platforms that also populate the social media ecosystem including Google+, YouTube, Instagram (one of the fastest-growing social platforms among teens), Pinterest (if you're into fashion or cooking, you might well be an avid "pinner"), Vine, Snapchat, and too many others to list here without making this a really tedious read.

Keeping in mind this growth, and also considering the numerous pundits who have argued that the potential for social media as a marketing platform is overstated,[1] there are three fundamental reasons why we believe social media represent a fundamental tool that organizations, companies, and brands must understand and learn to apply and leverage within their overall business approach to be successful in the years to come.

First, consumers (yes, *your* customers) are changing, fast. As mentioned earlier, we (yes, *we* are customers too!) demand more and more from the brands and companies with which we do business. Through sophisticated e-commerce platforms, we comparison shop in our pajamas at home or in the store, perhaps at the local Best Buy, comparing prices in real time with other online and offline retailers. We no longer attend to commercial messages as we did in the golden years of television. In fact, we place much more credibility on our peers' and friends' recommendations of products and services than we do on traditional advertising, and in many cases these recommendations and reviews take place online, fueled by Yelp, Facebook, Twitter, TripAdvisor, and others. And, the U.S. population, coincident with the aging baby boomer generation, is also expanding with a growing population of young people through the year 2050.[2] We call this Generation M3, for millennials, mobiles, and multitaskers, all raised and socialized in a time during which advances in the way we communicate via wireless technology and social media platforms have revolutionized the way we live, communicate, socialize, and shop.

Second, your competition isn't getting any easier. Scott Bedbury, in his book *A New Brand World*, talks about the commodification of undifferentiated and increasingly parity-like products and services and the challenge this presents to companies and their brands.[3] Whereas his book was written prior to the emergence of social media, its premise remains as valid as ever—that brands can and need to differentiate themselves based on communicating with consumers on levels defined by both functionality as well as emotions. Today, what better way to either jumpstart or maintain that function- and emotion-driven communication than with social media?

Third, based on our conversations and work with numerous advertising agencies and their clients, in part through our innovative M-School program initiative at Loyola Marymount University (LMU), we've seen that the pressure to justify marketing spending expenditure is increasing—exponentially. In other words, what used to be more of an art or a guessing game in terms of establishing your return on advertising investment (ROAI) has now become a science. Digital and social media generate a *huge* volume of data that can and should be harnessed and analyzed such that it provides a sustainable competitive advantage to companies able to do so. In this book, we aim to provide you an analytics framework and perspective with which to do this.

Who We Are

So who are we and what do we know about social media and its marketing applications and potential?

Michael Weiss is an Internet veteran. He started playing around with the Arpanet on his father's Digital computer (the VT220 with a 240-baud modem) in the early '80s. His father was a vice president at Digital Equipment Corporation (at one time, the second biggest computer company in the world—gone but not forgotten); so Michael and his brother hopped on their father's computer and spent their afternoons bothering operators on the network. As a teenager and into his 20s, he left the computer behind and focused solely on becoming a rock star. It was as the lead singer and bassist for a power pop trio in Boston that Weiss began to understand the power of social and word-of-mouth marketing. Write a great song, put on a great performance, spread the word, and the fans will come. While he never reached actual rock star fame, Weiss performed in front of thousands of people for most of the '80s and '90s. Flash forward to 1997 when he started one of the first digital agencies on the West Coast and remained the CEO for 14 years. Working with clients such as Disney, Estee Lauder, General Electric (GE), Fox, and hundreds of others, Weiss honed his skills as a digital marketer. In 2011, he stepped down as CEO and focused his career solely on working with brands to help them better understand what they want to be, who they want to target, and how to use digital and online social platforms to engage audiences. In 2014, Weiss married his love of rock and roll and marketing by becoming the VP of marketing for Musician's Friend, one of the largest online musical retailers in the world; and he has since become a seasoned TEDx Talker, which is almost like becoming a rock star.

Andy Rohm is an associate professor in the Marketing Department at LMU in Los Angeles and director of LMU's M-School, a new and innovative undergraduate educational initiative designed to transform higher learning in the area of digital and social media marketing (see blogs.lmu. edu/mschool). He is also an ex-aerospace engineer (really) who, right out of college, worked at large companies selling complex products Pratt & Whitney and services (General Motors and EDS) and who experienced his first midlife crisis in his late 20s and moved to the Australian outback to play cowboy and pick mangos. After countless mosquito bites and Vegemite sandwiches, Rohm moved back to the United States where he shifted careers to the athletic footwear industry, working in sales and marketing positions at Brooks Sports and Reebok International. Presenting marketing and new product launch plans to salespeople and retail buyers became so much fun that he decided to go back to school, earn his PhD in Marketing at the University of Massachusetts Amherst, and begin conducting exciting research and teaching courses in the area of new media, first at Northeastern University in Boston and then at LMU. Professor Rohm's social media experience not only comes from his cutting-edge research and teaching in the M-School program, but also from seeing his children grow up as digital natives in a hyperconnected world.

Our motivation in writing this book is to provide strategic and timeless insights and fundamentals that will help you and your organization, company, or brand develop and manage your social media marketing efforts. These fundamentals include:

- Understanding the importance of being able to define your organization's purpose and key objectives based on what it stands for
- Understanding your customer and developing a content marketing strategy that communicates your "story" based on the online social channels where she or he is active

- Understanding how to generate consumer insights from your online social dialogue
- Defining your key performance indicators (KPIs) and in turn generating relevant analytics that help align your organization's or brand's success against key measures

In short, this book is intended to provide you (whether an upper-level undergraduate or MBA student, social media manager, brand manager, small business owner, corporate executive, or simply someone who wishes to better understand the intersection of business and social media) much-needed perspectives and frameworks on developing and managing an effective social media strategy and presence. In doing so, we've sought to leverage our extensive industry experience, based on our industry work along with our current and original research conducted in the field of social media marketing, to help you cut through the noise, static, and confusion respective to the social media landscape and to enable you to develop and communicate a well-thought-out, cohesive, and strategic approach to social media marketing.

We're glad you're here, and we hope you take away some important lessons and insights from this book regarding a strategic approach to harnessing the power of social media marketing.

Michael and Andy
Herdingcatsbook.com

CHAPTER 1

Who Are You and Why Should We Care?

If you were born and raised in the precommercial Internet era, particularly during the 1960s and 1970s, you most likely grew up watching TV shows like the *Beverly Hillbillies, Happy Days*, or *M*A*S*H* and reading newspapers that were delivered to your parents' front porch by the newspaper boy (what a quaint notion—having your morning or afternoon paper delivered by the enterprising kid down the block). If you did watch lots of TV, your programming most likely came from the three major networks—CBS, NBC, and ABC. All this made advertisers' lives, especially media planners' jobs, pretty swell.

To reach consumers and generate awareness, interest, or desire in your brand, and depending of course on their budget, all they had to do was develop a television commercial, a newspaper or magazine ad, a billboard execution, or advertise in the Yellow Pages. Because we didn't have TiVo or digital video recorders (DVRs) back then, we had no recourse but to watch (or ignore) ads on TV. Many of us didn't even have remote controls until the 1980s; so unless we wanted to get up off the couch and physically change the channel, we just sat there and actually tuned into commercials. And, our phones were actually used for making phone calls! Caller ID? We had to answer the phone to find out if we wanted to talk with the person on the other end.

Yet if you were born after the mid-1980s or in the 1990s, you're reading this section as if you were reading your high school history book. And chances are you are reading it on a mobile device. The point is, the past 30 years (we'll use 1982 and the launch of MTV as a reference point) have brought about amazing changes and shifts in the sheer volume of commercial media available and the way we consume it. As consumers, we have evolved and now expect a lot from companies and their brands, and in the true sense of instant gratification, we want it *now*! Moreover, if we don't find brands' messages interesting or relevant or funny, we are more able than ever to tune it out. In a recent article illustrating the concept of the social media ecosystem, the paper's authors argue that "Consumers are no longer content with advertising as a bystander sport…Consumers now expect [and demand] to be active participants in the media process."[1] The fact that we are no longer content to passively consume whatever content brands broadcast to us means that companies and advertisers must be much more innovative, creative, and accepting of risk than ever before to generate awareness, engagement, and advocacy.

Experts have called this the *attention economy*, the *me generation*, or (parents, you'll love this one) simply the age of the *spoiled and entitled consumer*. Our behavior and expectations, combined with fast-evolving media technologies, force these brands in turn to work even harder than ever to reach us with advertising content that we'll take note of and attend to. The result? Companies and consumers alike soon become overwhelmed with the explosion of media platforms and the cacophony of messages out there, vying for our attention.

In this chapter, we argue that to stand out and stand apart amidst this chaotic landscape of media and messages, you first must look inward and understand *who you are as a brand, a company, or an organization, and why you do what you do*. By doing so, you develop and present a clarity and uniqueness that will enable you to not only convey your unique point of difference (POD) to your consumers, but will additionally make the task of navigating what we call *POEM*—Paid media such as television, print, and banner ads; Owned media such as your firm's website and Facebook presence; Earned media such as shares, comments, posts, repins, and retweets; and the M stands for media—easier.

We'll tap into several useful frameworks and perspectives for better understanding your brand's or organization's unique POD as well as for better understanding your customers and your relationship with them. These frameworks and perspectives include the Golden Circle, demographic versus psychographic customer profiles, the functional as well as the emotional characteristics of your product or service offering, customer pain points, and customer need states and motivations. Let's start with the *why*, as in "why do we exist as a brand, a company, or organization?"

The *Why*

Simon Sinek, in his widely viewed Ted Talk featuring the "Golden Circle" concept,[2] poses a simple yet important question to managers and executives: What is the *why* that lies behind those successful companies or organizations that lead their industries? In other words, in an existential sense, the question is analogous to "why is your company in business and why should anyone care?" Sinek's Golden Circle is made up of an outer circle (what you do), a concentric middle circle (how you do it), and an inner, bull's-eye circle (why you do it).

He begins his talk with the example of a well-known brand—the *what*, *how*, and *why* of Apple. Apple's *what* is that it designs and markets desktop computers, laptops, phones, and other devices. The *how* involves Apple's sourcing and marketing prowess and its manufacturing partners. The *why*—well, that's where Sinek argues that Apple really gets it in terms of identifying its *raison d'etre* and why its products stand out vis-á-vis its competition. Sinek argues that if Apple was like other brands, it would pompously state that "we make great computers…want to buy one?" and be done with it. And this is how most marketing and social media is done. In contrast, Sinek goes on to say that Apple's *why* is that everything the company does challenges the status quo; that at Apple innovation comes first, and secondarily, it just happens to make great computers and devices. Another great example of the Golden Circle is how Starbucks views its brand. Howard Schultz, Starbucks CEO, once remarked that one of his employees proposed Starbucks' *why* as this: That Starbucks is not in the coffee business serving people, yet rather is in the *people* business serving *coffee*.[3] This fits well to Starbucks' positioning as "the third place," that place where people go and hang out outside of the home and the office, similar to the quintessential Irish pub.

What does Sinek's Golden Circle have to do with social media marketing and brand building? Everything. This chapter presents an important platform for thinking about, developing, and managing your organization's social media strategy, one that is centered on the *why* concept and truly thinking about why your company or organization exists (its brand DNA), and further why you get out of bed in the morning to help lead that organization. Once you are able to move beyond the *what* of what you do on a daily basis (whether it's to design and sell laptops and mobile devices or rid homes of termites) and the *how* of how you do it, you can begin to craft your *why*, your own unique story, and this enables you to begin thinking about how that story might be told, retold, and shared via social media.

Action Step #1

Think about some of your most admired or favorite brands in addition to Apple, whether it's Nike, Virgin America, method, TOMS Shoes, Betabrand, or others. What is their respective *why*? Then, think about your company—what does it represent, what does it stand for, and what is its brand DNA? If you don't know why you do what you do, and particularly if your social media presence isn't able to communicate this, then how will your customers know? This type of exercise makes for a great company-wide brainstorming session—after all, how often do you and your colleagues truly take the time to reflect on what your company stands for and why you're in business?

So, Who Are You?

No really, *who are you*? According to the terrific book on generating consumer insights titled *Hitting the Sweet Spot*,[4] if you were to answer this question in marketing speak, you might say: I am a 25 to 34 year urban male in a DINK (dual income no kids) relationship with a HHI of $75,000+ and a moderate-to-high disposable income. I drive a premium-class SUV, dine out two to four times per week, and play video games five or more times per week. And, I am a low-to-moderate consumer within the fast-food category. Yet, to what extent does this description, one that attempts to define us in preset categories and demographics, *really* define who you are as a unique individual?

In response to the question "tell me about yourself" at a cocktail party or a job interview, how would you describe yourself? Would you describe yourself as belonging to certain demographics-defined categories or would you attempt to paint a more intimate or engaging personal portrait? After all, our parents did in fact tell us at a young age that we were truly one of a kind. If you were to answer the same question in a way that *really* communicates who you are and what gets you out of bed in the morning, you might have answered it a bit differently: I love waking up early to walk my black Lab, I sometimes eat too many French fries in one sitting, I can't sit still in meetings, and I can't wait to go bike riding in Provence next summer. Oh, and I lose my keys…all the time.

Whereas the first approach in defining your consumer—who, in fact, is indeed a unique individual—based on demographics is factual and accurate, if you were to truly differentiate yourself as the unique individual that you are, the second approach based on psychographics is much more descriptive to anyone wanting to get to know you on a personal level. Now, work to apply this same mindset to your company's or brand's customers and your social media presence, the space where your brand conveys the functional and emotional promise that your product or service delivers.

For instance, imagine you're the founder of a small business—we'll call it Catch-A-Treat—producing and selling gluten-free, surfboard-shaped dog bones. To position your company as a small- to medium-sized business competing within the premium, organic dog treat category would be accurate. And, that positioning places you in a multibillion dollar (and growing) industry. Yet is that really enough to set your company or brand apart from your (most likely thousands of) competitors? Taking this example even further, you could even define the essence of your Catch-A-Treat brand as one that symbolizes healthy, fun, surf-inspired snacks for dogs and their owners who believe that their beloved pooch deserves more than just the standard dog bone. After all, marketing scholars have described brands and their products (such as dog bones) as "nothing more than an artifact around which customers have experiences."[5] If you're a dog owner, you might well be able to relate. If you're not, talk to some friends who are dog owners about their attachment to their furry friends—you'll perhaps be surprised at the seemingly irrational connection they've forged with their dog (or cat).

Taking this example one step further yet, imagine how this emotionally charged positioning (for instance, the Catch-A-Treat story) could be effectively and efficiently communicated via social media platforms such as Facebook, YouTube, Instagram, Pinterest, Vine, Snapchat, and others, where the medium itself is by nature more intimate and social than traditional communication platforms ever could be. By thinking closely and deeply about who you are and what your organization or brand represents, you are one step closer to defining your *why*.

Why Should We Care?

Why is it so important to define and stress over your company's or organization's *why*? Remember, we interact and become engaged with companies and their products and services because they have something to offer. That new toothpaste you bought promises to whiten your teeth better than your previous brand. That new SUV offers the all-important third row of seats for those school carpool pickups and drop-offs. That new pair of running shoes comes with a glowing review in *Runner's World* magazine. In short, we care because brands and their associated products or services help us solve our problems and fill our unmet needs or wants.

Let's back up a bit. The American Marketing Association (AMA) defines marketing as "the activity, set of institutions, and processes for creating, communicating, delivering, and exchanging offerings that have value for customers, clients, partners, and society at large."[6] We prefer a simpler definition—*marketing is about finding out what people are putting up with and solving it*. Eric Johnson, founder of the advertising agency Ignited, calls this helping to solve our *pain points*—those things in life that bother us, that get in the way of the perfect day, or that simply annoy us. In consumer behavior research, these pain points represent the gap between our ideal states as consumers and individuals and our actual states, those states of being that we have to put up with in an imperfect world. What are your pain points? Better yet, what are the pain points of your customers that your company seeks to address?

Once you begin to identify and address those consumer pain points, you are one step closer to identifying your role in your customers' daily lives.

In a recent undergraduate marketing class offered within our M-School program at LMU, we conducted an exercise that had our students identify their own pain points, and we were surprised by the emotions behind some of the answers, including chipped nail polish, boyfriends, rude people, slow downloads, and slow checkout lines in the grocery store. Really—chipped nail polish? But to our upper level undergraduates (aged 20 to 22), the seemingly random life issues they brought up were truly pain points to them in that these issues actually induced some level of social and psychic pain. By being able to identify and understand what your customers are putting up with or dealing with in their lives or careers, you are one important step closer to crafting a meaningful, relevant, and engaging social media presence.

Another colleague, former athletic footwear guru and marketing expert, Tom Carmody, developed his own simple framework for marketers seeking to help address individuals' pain points: FANAFI.

Find
A
Need
And
Fill
It

The FANAFI framework is a brilliantly simple model for companies seeking to better understand their unique (and hopefully defensible) selling point in their respective market. It poses the question, "What is it that we do that will make our customers lives better?" Prior to the FANAFI framework and the concept of pain points, the well-known psychologist, Abraham Maslow, developed his pyramid-shaped hierarchy[7] to illustrate the need states that individuals seek to attain, including the lower level states of physical safety and security along with higher level need states such as self-image, prestige, status, and belonging.

Maslow's Hierarchy of Human Needs

In our work and teaching, we've found that Maslow's hierarchy of human needs is a relevant framework with which to map out the reasons why prospective customers become loyal customers—because your product or service meets one or more of the higher level needs defined by Maslow. For instance, most cars manufactured today function pretty well and almost all have good safety or quality ratings and warranties. Yet some car brands are able to command premium prices and premium margins. Why? See Maslow for the answer. While the price of admission in the car industry is a good-quality car that comes with a warranty and attractive styling, premium brands such as BMW, Mercedes-Benz, and Lexus, among others, appeal to those higher level needs highlighted by Maslow.

The point here is that by identifying your *why* and your customers' pain points, you begin to define the ways that you can connect with consumers via social media on functional levels of relevance and usefulness as well as deeper, emotional levels of self-identity reaffirmation, ego, status, prestige, belonging, and even self-actualization (when it comes to taking care of our beloved pets, for instance). After all, your brand is more than merely a two-dimensional logo—it's a symbol that instills confidence, reputation, and personality in terms of characteristics such as sincerity, excitement, competence, sophistication, or ruggedness. And all this leads to consumer familiarity, preference, and loyalty.

Here's a second action step, also ideal for a company brainstorming session, designed to identify what your consumers are putting up with and how you can help.

Action Step #2

In another brainstorming session, particularly with your employees doing battle on the front lines (for instance, your sales and customer service reps), identify the various pain points that your prospective and current customers are putting up with related to your products or services. Now, define the emotional drivers or needs associated with these pain points and how your products or services can help address and alleviate them. Then, begin to think about how you might begin to engage your social media to communicate this.

Social Media and Intimacy

Our main point thus far is that the first step in *strategically* developing or reassessing your brand's social media strategy is to back up and think hard about what your company or organization stands for and why it exists. The mistake many firms make is that they view social media as a channel to merely generate "likes," followers, and even immediate sales by delivering discounts and other price incentives to prospective or current customers.[8]

Of course in the short term, this approach may help generate traffic in your store or restaurant or visits to your website. And, it may lead to increased revenues, albeit at the risk of diminishing margins. In the longer term, however, unless you're Amazon or Costco and can compete effectively with both razor-thin margins *and* scale, competing on price may not be an effective strategy for you over time.

In a strategic sense, view your social media platforms as a way to not only promote and provide direct incentives, but also as an intimate setting (kind of like a campfire) to creatively involve and engage your customers with your company or brand story. In the next two chapters (Customer Engagement and Storytelling), we highlight how and why both small and large firms employ this approach in using social media to better connect with customers.

Action Step #3

We hope this chapter has provided insights and ways of thinking about your company, your organization, your brand, and your *why*. In the following chapters, we introduce and bring clarity to the concept of consumer engagement and how it relates to social media, and present a timeless framework for crafting your story and engaging your customers. Your third action step for this chapter is to craft a *why* manifesto for your organization based on action step #1 (your *why*) and action step #2 (identifying and addressing customer pain points). Your *why* manifesto could read something like this:

For [your target consumer] that puts up with [pain point], our [brand, product, service] is a [your solution to the pain point] that [the emotional benefit to your customer]. Unlike the competition, [our brand, product and service] is [unique differentiator].

Most importantly, dig deep into your brand's or organization's *why* while crafting your manifesto. It will pay off in the long run!

The Insider's Perspective

Eric Johnson, Founder and President, Ignited Advertising

In our work with brands such as the U.S. Army and DTS, we first begin with a process of identifying the *why* behind what the company does and what the brand stands for. For instance, with our client DTS (DTS develops and produces sound technologies for professional and consumer use, at dts.com), we put together a series of workshops to get at that unique point of difference or positioning that defines the DTS brand. As a result of this process, we came up with a positioning platform for DTS called "Sound Matters," based on the insight that *sound changes the way we see*. By working through this process, we were able to help DTS more effectively position itself in a very competitive industry and create more compelling branded content that could be communicated across multiple channels, including online and social media.

CHAPTER 2

Customer Engagement

In a landmark 1960s Supreme Court ruling on pornography and free speech, Justice Potter Stewart famously stated, in the Court's efforts and attempts to define obscenity, "I know it when I see it."[1] The same challenge applies to defining the concept of *customer engagement*.

Both industry experts and marketing scholars offer widely differing views of what customer engagement is. For instance, in 2006, the Advertising Research Foundation proposed an initial definition of customer engagement as the process of "turning on a prospect to a brand idea enhanced by the surrounding context." A more practical definition of customer engagement by Wikipedia states that it "is the engagement of customers with one another, with a company or a brand. The initiative for engagement can be either consumer- or company-led and the medium of engagement can be on or offline." And in the academic literature, customer engagement has been defined as "a customer's behavioral manifestation toward a brand or firm" and that it "results from motivational drivers, manifested in customer purchasing behavior, the acquisition of new customers through promotions and referrals programs, customers' influence of other consumers through word-of-mouth activity, and customer feedback provided to the firm."[2]

Whatever the definition, we argue that the concept itself, one of interacting and connecting with consumers in meaningful and relevant ways, is paramount in today's chaotic and cluttered world saturated with commercial messages. Applying Justice Stewart's approach to the Supreme Court's attempt to define obscenity, we recognize customer engagement when we simply walk into an Apple retail store and are met by a friendly Apple associate with her mobile device in hand. We experience the concept of customer engagement when we enter a Niketown and are immediately surrounded by the sights and sounds that define the Nike brand.

We recognize customer engagement when we enter the clothing company Betabrand's website and become immersed in the humorous, irreverent, and tongue-in-cheek descriptions of the various Betabrand apparel items, ranging from the crotch heat index "research" used to describe the benefits of its Cordaround pants to its disco ball-themed athletic shorts. Perhaps most central to this book, we experience customer engagement when a customer tweets or posts a comment or question on your company's or brand's Twitter or Facebook page and you actually reply, in a timely and thoughtful fashion.

What Is Customer Engagement?

Our objective in this chapter is not merely to provide a working definition of customer engagement. Perhaps more importantly, our objective is to show you how and why social media platforms such as Facebook, Twitter, Instagram, and others are central to helping organizations and companies engage effectively with their customers. In doing so, we tap into research conducted by one of the authors to illustrate the role of social media in fostering and maintaining company–customer engagement. One of the authors recently conducted a study of college undergraduate and graduate students and how they interacted with various brands via specific social media platforms on a daily basis over time.[3]

The student participants in the study were directed to keep a diary documenting their social media interactions with a brand of their choice via three platforms (Facebook, Twitter, and e-mail) over a one-week period. Overall, we analyzed over 300 discrete brand–customer interactions. We found that the brand interactions on Facebook and Twitter were classified by five primary motives for engaging with the specific brand: (1) for accessing product or service information, (2) for accessing fresh and timely content, (3) for accessing fun and entertaining content, (4) to provide feedback and ideas related to products, services, and branded content, and (5) for issues related to customer service.

Integrating the managerial and academic literature and layering on our industry experience and research findings, we therefore define customer engagement as a state in which individuals move past a level of awareness with your company or brand—an awareness that your organization simply exists—to the stage where they interact with your company or brand, online or offline, through the following five actions:

1. Consuming content such as videos or postings related to your company or brand
2. Posting content (yes, both positive and negative)
3. Sharing and forwarding content
4. Recommending and referring others to your company or brand
5. Providing product and service feedback and ideas and cocreating brand meaning

Further, we propose that company–customer engagement is primarily motivated by both functional (e.g., for product or service information) as well as hedonic and emotional drivers (e.g., for fun, for entertainment, for prestige, or social currency).

To begin, let's start with a principle from the advertising and sales management literature that we'll call the A-I-D-C framework. This framework illustrates four stages of how we respond to advertising or other persuasive messages: attention, interest, desire, and conviction. The A(ttention) stage is analogous to your ability to simply establish company or brand awareness, to enter the consumer's radar screen. Specific to the world of social media, brands gain attention through surface-level actions such as generating Facebook likes, getting noticed via sponsored Facebook posts or banner ads, generating views of a branded YouTube video, and through Twitter posts.

The I(nterest) and D(esire) stages are where things become interesting for you and your customer. This is the stage where you become part of the consumer's consideration set, where you've said or done or offered something that has captured their attention. Moreover, this is the stage where customer engagement begins. Back to the previous example, at this stage, consumers' interest might be illustrated by the overall time spent viewing a video about your brand posted on your website or on YouTube, sharing the video with friends, sharing the brand's Facebook post, or retweeting a tweet from or about your brand. Finally, the C(onviction) stage that follows is where your social media efforts directly influence your customer to buy or take some other purchase- or transaction-related action, online or off.

Action Step #1

Develop a social media audit where you map your organization's level of social engagement (on a scale of 1 to 5, where 1 = no engagement and 5 = significant engagement) based on the five types identified in this section: *consuming content* related to your company or brand, *posting content* (positive and negative), *sharing and forwarding content, recommending and referring* others to your company or brand, and *providing product and service feedback and ideas*. In the areas where you score less than a 3, identify ways, including the use of additional social platforms beyond the ones you are currently employing, to foster greater engagement in these areas.

A New Twist to Customer Engagement

Imagine that you're a 17 year-old soon-to-be high school graduate on the market for a used car. Or, you've received your first paycheck from that dishwashing gig at the local restaurant and you finally have some disposable income to dispose of or at least place in a savings account. Further, up to this point in your life, institutions such as banks that can help you do these things have been merely impersonal, perhaps intimidating, places that your parents and other "older" people frequent. From your perspective, not only do you not understand how they operate, you don't have a clue as to which bank you might want to use to apply for a used car loan or with which to simply open a savings account.

This was the case facing the global bank, Rabobank, in 2008 as it faced stiff competition in the European retail banking category. Financial institutions such as Rabobank are part of a complex and global service industry and, often, younger prospective customers are either uneducated about the services offered by financial institutions or are unwilling to use them because they are confused with the complexity of services offered. What does this have to do with social media? In response to the challenge of connecting with younger customers, Rabobank worked with a third-party firm to develop a social, online persona, or online agent, named Yvette, to assist younger or prospective customers in their dealings and relationships with the bank. Yvette's online persona was portrayed as a young Dutch woman who represented the bank. Moreover, she (better yet, her digital persona) was active in social media with a Hyves profile (at the time, the Dutch equivalent of Facebook).

Yvette's interactions with current as well as prospective bank customers took place in an online chat forum that was part of the bank's website. Although online agents such as Yvette are nothing new (for instance, the retailer IKEA has an online agent named Anna to help answer shoppers' questions, and the U.S. Army employs an online agent named Sgt. Star to assist potential recruits with enlistment information and advice), Yvette is different. She was developed to not only *react* to questions posed by individuals, similar to an FAQ question-and-response interface, she was also programmed with the unique ability to be *proactive* in her current interactions based on content captured from previous interactions. She was also developed to deliver both *functional* content in her interactions (for instance, how to apply for a used car loan at the bank, what identification one would need to open up a savings account) as well as content that is more *social* in nature. For example, after an individual opened up a chat session with her, Yvette might ask, "How is your day going?" in a reactive manner, or she might ask proactively, "How was your trip to Barcelona last month?" In short, she was developed to be able to tap into past interaction content to be proactive in her conversations with individuals, yet she was also developed to interact socially with the individual in addition to conveying functional information related to the bank.

One of the authors worked on an in-depth study of the effectiveness of Yvette as an online socialization agent, an agent able to interact with and engage customers socially and proactively as well as functionally and reactively.[4] What we found was that whereas Yvette's ability to deliver functional content in her customer–bank interactions was important, it was her ability to engage customers initially in a social manner, which led to her effectiveness as an online socialization agent of the bank. We also found that Yvette's effectiveness was accelerated by her ability to be proactive rather than merely reactive. In other words, her proactive interactions (e.g., when she initiated a conversation thread or was able to tap into previous interaction content) positively influenced levels of customer engagement when combined with the appropriate content (social or functional). In terms of company metrics, our findings revealed that interactions with Yvette resulted in a number of positive outcomes for the bank, including account activity leading to increased account revenues.

What this means to you is that online agents don't necessarily have to serve as mere FAQ advisors. These agents can be both proactive and social in helping consumers become more familiar or comfortable in doing business with your company or organization. Yet, we're pretty sure you're asking yourself right now, "OK, but who in their right mind would actually carry on a social interaction with an online agent, even if she is an attractive Dutch woman named Yvette?" Our reply would be, and is, that the younger "digital natives" that are or soon will be an important part of your customer funnel might actually prefer to interact with an online, rather than a human, agent in service settings such as banks.[5] We also argue that these digital natives, those born and raised during the late 1990s and 2000s, are socialized to view what constitutes a "friend" differently than us "more mature" types who know what a pay phone is and remember typing college term papers on a typewriter.

Social Media-Fueled Customer Engagement

The Rabobank and Yvette example illustrates how important it is to look beyond effective social media marketing as merely developing and executing a Facebook, Twitter, Instagram, or Pinterest strategy. The *social* in social media implies that brands and organizations must take a step back and consider mediums and platforms that enable two things: a seat at the dinner party and a story to tell, one that is relevant, compelling, and sharable. Furthermore, it's important that you ask yourself two salient questions:

1. Where do your current and prospective customers live online?
2. What social currency do you own that aligns with these online platforms?

For example, if you are starting a travel blog and want to develop a following, which could lead to advertising revenue on your blog, you might recognize that your actual and prospective customers might be avid Pinterest or Instagram users who also depend on TripAdvisor for planning trips and vacations. With this in mind, your social currency as an up-and-coming travel blogger is one of uncovering unique or undiscovered destinations for your readers. Aligning this travel currency with social media, services such as Pinterest and Instagram or Vine would offer ideal platforms with which to repurpose your blog content in the form of pictures and short video format. Another example of social media engagement is how the Ruthie Davis shoe brand (ruthiedavis.com) has grown in popularity among celebrities and fashionistas, including Lady Gaga, Beyonce, Halle Berry, and many others. According to Ruthie, building customer or "fan" engagement via social media such as Facebook, Twitter, Instagram, Tumblr, and Pinterest has been critical to her success. How does she do it? By capturing and curating organic content that represents the core of the Ruthie Davis brand (its *why*) and distributing that content strategically across her social channels.

The challenge many social media practitioners face, and the trap they fall in to, however, is that they treat all platforms equally. After all, they're all social media, aren't they? Well, yes and no. A simple and effective way of looking at the issue of aligning your social currency with the right social media platform (whether it be Twitter or Facebook or Pinterest or Vine or some yet-to-be-developed platform) is to think of your options in terms of two unique dimensions (what we love to call a 2 × 2 matrix in academic speak and what industry folks love to call a framework): *intimacy* and *content*.

The *intimacy dimension* differentiates social media platforms based on the extent to which they help to foster a relatively close connection among users. The *content dimension* differentiates platforms based on the type of content they convey. For instance, while Facebook has more than one billion registered users around the globe, it also creates a perceived level of intimacy among users that are part of a network of friends or groups. Both Facebook and LinkedIn users can be segmented into close-knit groups based on characteristics such as school attended, work-related community, and many other segmentation factors. Thus, both platforms offer marketers the opportunity to communicate with narrow segments. In terms of content, though, a platform such as Facebook delivers it via the written word, via photos, through video, and increasingly via our smartphone (on an average, people spend significantly more time on Facebook via their mobile phone than they do through their desktop).

Hence, Facebook has been able to maintain its dominance as the social "go to" platform for individuals worldwide.

However, if you're a 14 year-old girl living in Santa Monica, a more personal platform for you to communicate with your friends might be Instagram, Pinterest, or Snapchat, where your pictures or videos (the content) portray a more intimate side of you than mere postings and standard photos. For Rabobank, the social platform chosen to provide the bank its desired social currency was Hyves. For your company, perhaps it's one or more of the major platforms in existence today, or perhaps it hasn't yet been created. There lies the importance of looking beyond platform-specific strategies to first starting with the question of how can you best engage your audience.

Action Step #2

Now it's your turn to develop an intimacy and content map. Create an Intimacy × Content matrix for your organization, mapping the type of content you are seeking to convey with the social media platform that best fits that content in fostering a closer connection with your customers.

Customer Engagement: The DNA of Effective Social Media Strategy

In the first chapter, we discussed the concept of brand DNA and the importance of determining what it is it that defines your company, organization, or brand (your *why*). In this chapter, we argue that customer engagement is the centerpiece, the DNA, of your social media strategy. By first identifying your *raison d'etre* (loosely translated as follows: If your company or organization suddenly disappeared in the middle of the night, would anyone miss it?), the next step is to think of ways to engage your audience via social media platforms, given, of course, your reason for being—your *why*.

We cannot emphasize enough how important these first two steps are to defining your approach to successfully employing social media as a marketing communications and sales tool. Using Facebook as an example of social media-fueled engagement, when one of your customers likes your Facebook page, it begins the wheel of influence with your customer's friends in terms of brand or company recall and even purchase intent.

In closing, a timeless approach to engaging engage people is to tell them a story. From the fairy tales your mom and dad read to you as a kid to the late Elmore Leonard's mysteries and thrillers to the Hunger Games series to the Harlequin romance novels where the man and woman fall in love and live happily ever after, we all relate to storytelling. We relate to stories because we cast ourselves in the story's narrative, where these narratives can convey ideal life states and outcomes (true and everlasting love), help us solve life's challenges (social acceptance, belonging, and fitting in), or simply provide us an escape from reality. So, even before you begin to create and curate the content (postings, tweets, videos) that drives your social media presence, begin to apply the storytelling perspective in your content strategy. After all, you do want to engage your audience, don't you? And this is what Chapter 3 is all about—crafting and telling your unique story.

The Insider's Perspective

Niki Weber, former senior vice president, Global Integrated Marketing, Quiksilver

Herding, uniting, combining, joining, and bridging communities and passion points are all critical behaviors to any good social, digital, and engagement strategy. At Quiksilver Inc., we compete in the mountains, the waves, and the city. Our beautiful playground enables us to generate lots of amazing visual content and stories. This leads to Facebook, Instagram, YouTube, and Twitter serving as key social platforms for us. As social media matures, though, it's also important to know with *absolute precision* what social levers to pull, and when to pull them, to foster engagement, especially as the options and the available data sources grow and become overwhelming. Developing and executing a social media strategy can be a huge time suck and a "quality of work diffuser" if you're not careful. It's like you're Indiana Jones in *The Last Crusade* trying to figure out which goblet to drink from, without getting killed, all the while herding cats of all breeds (the myriad social platforms) going in all sorts of directions.

CHAPTER 3

It's Story Time!

Admit it—ultimately we're all in the business of persuasion. Whether you're a salesperson, a teacher, a parent, a manager, a spouse, or significant other, aren't you always trying to persuade someone else to do something? Persuading people to do something different is what we do—to get them go to the movie *we* want to see, to get that report in on time, to revise the creative that your team has been working on for three weeks, to go to *that* restaurant, or to vacation near Pebble Beach rather than Disney World. Or, in the mindset of an advertising or marketing person, to get people to buy your new product, buy more of your current product, or switch from a competing brand to yours.

One tried-and-true pathway to persuasion is to engage people in a story. Why? Because through stories and the related narrative, we become interested and engaged, and we process the message and the content contained within the story more willingly. Some have described storytelling as the "ultimate mashup of ancient traditions and new communication models."[1] Around campfires, during long car rides, even on the walls of caves during the Aurignacian cultural period more than 25,000 years ago, storytelling has long been a central way of communicating.

In his book *Start Something That Matters*, the founder of TOMS Shoes and its "One for One Giving Program," Blake Mycoskie states that "A good story transcends boundaries, breaks barriers, opens doors. It is a key not only to starting a business but also clarifying your own personal identity and choices."[2] Mycoskie compares modern-day brands such as method (the ecofriendly cleaning products company spelled with a small "m"), and its ability to craft a compelling story about what the method brand stands for, with the more traditional approach to advertising portrayed on the television show *Mad Men* where brands were sold to us with unilateral messages about why they were so great and wonderful. Mycoskie goes on to argue that the old-school approach to marketing and advertising simply does not cut it today with our increasingly complex and fragmented media ecosystem consisting of digital, social, broadcast, and numerous other media platforms.

As highlighted in the previous chapter, we all relate to stories—fairy tales, mysteries, myths, and suspense novels—whereby many of these stories feature one simple common element—the concept of the hero, the protagonist who we feel for and who we want to see succeed. Central to this book, the one thing about good stories is that we like to share them with others.

Today, though, the telling of a story can be more complex than simply scratching charcoal on the wall of a cave or gathering friends around a campfire. The explosion of different forms of online and offline media, including social media, makes effective storytelling a much more complex task. Yet, given the rapid changes in communication platforms and technologies, the central point remains: We are hardwired to listen to, to tell, and to respond to content presented to us in story format.

Action Step #1

Drawing from Dr. Lisa Fortini-Campbell's book *Hitting the Sweet Spot,*[3] here is a quick exercise that we run with our undergraduate M-School students at LMU that helps show them that they are actually pretty decent persuaders and also what made their successful persuasive attempts successful. Try it with *your* team and apply the insights generated to *your* brand:

1. Think of three recent persuasion attempts by you that were successful and three that were not. These persuasive efforts could be related to your colleagues at work, children, spouses and significant others, friends, or even strangers.
2. Next, think about what it was about your successful attempts that made them so successfully persuasive and also think about your not-so-successful attempts; what seemed to be the dynamics taking place in both?
3. Create a list of insights that came from both the positive and negative attempts. Specifically, what was it that made your successful attempts so successful? What seemed to be lacking in your not-so-successful attempts?

What you might find is that your successful attempts tapped into some of the secrets of good storytelling: seeing things from the other person's point of view, creating a level of excitement or tension or adventure, recognizing that people deep down generally like to be consistent in their actions and beliefs, and employing metaphors and comparisons to describe what you are striving for in your persuasive attempt.

A great example of storytelling was seen in October 2012 when the Space Shuttle Endeavour was retired and towed night and day from Los Angeles International Airport to its final stop at the California Science Center. Many thought the process of towing it down streets populated with trees and cluttered with signs and electrical wires, and over the infamous 405 Freeway, would be just short of impossible. The hero of the story? The Endeavour of course. Yet another hero in the story was the Toyota Tundra, the pickup truck that pulled the Endeavour in a journey of a lifetime that was seen in person by thousands of people along the course and by millions of viewers online.

In their book *The Hero and The Outlaw: Building Extraordinary Brands Through the Power of Archetypes*, the authors Margaret Mark and Carol Pearson talk about creating effective brand narratives through establishing a brand hero (e.g, Nike), a brand outlaw (e.g., Harley-Davidson), or an all-knowing sage brand (e.g., IBM). The Red Bull Stratos space dive project in which skydiver Felix Baumgartner free-fell from 24 miles in the stratosphere and parachuted safely to terra firma is a textbook example of a compelling narrative that thrived on social media—complete with the technical difficulties and postponements that went along with the project and the risk of possible death that made it real. Effective brand narrative also taps into *brand headwind*—where the brand truly believes in and is fighting for something worth achieving.

Hamsters Rule Social Media

You might remember a television commercial from back in 2009 launching Kia's new Soul vehicle that portrayed three hipsterlike hamsters navigating a Soul around their less fortunate brethren stuck in numerous rodent rolling cages strewn throughout the street. As the *über*cool hamsters drive along the road in their new Soul, they open up the driver's side window to reveal the bass-heavy thump thump thump of some equally cool music coming from the car. The hamster driver looks out the open window, nods his head nonchalantly to his fellow hamster spinning mindlessly (and going nowhere) on its hamster wheel, and drives on. This commercial, by the Los Angeles-based agency David&Goliath titled "A New Way to Roll," provides a novel and unexpected narrative that connects with young car buyers and highlights the continued, and growing, importance of combining storytelling with advertising content. The campaign also fueled millions of YouTube views, fostered tens of thousands of fans on Facebook, and helped drive Kia's year-to-date sales up 45 percent in 2010.[4]

Yet, more important than its social presence, the theme of the Kia Soul story is a classic one—and one that seeks to position Kia effectively vis-á-vis its bigger and stronger (in terms of media spending) competition in a brand-as-outlaw mentality: don't simply follow the masses and do or buy what everyone else does; stand out, be different. This timeless theme, portrayed in past commercials such as Apple's famous "1984" spot, speaks to the common woman or man (hamsters, after all, albeit cute are pretty unremarkable rodents) who wants to have fun and be cool and speaks to the idea that "you, too, can be somebody."

Robert Rose and Joe Pulizzi write about the "brand hero's journey" in their book *Managing Content Marketing*[5] and the importance of creating your own brand story. And just like in any good story, the brand hero or protagonist becomes someone we root or feel for as it begins its journey (e.g., to make the world's best computer, to make driving fun again, to rid local homes of termites), encounters challenges along the way, and manages to overcome those challenges.

Storytelling's in Our DNA

In fact, experts argue that it's our natural tendency to be storytellers and to want to listen to stories. Why? Dr. Pamela Rutledge, Director of the Media Psychology Research Center, argues that stories

- have long been a primal form of interpersonal communication;
- engage us through emotions, trigger our imagination, and connect us with others;

- are how we think and organize our thoughts through schemas, scripts, mental models, or cognitive maps;
- are how we persuade others.

In other words, we're hardwired to listen to, to tell, and to process what we learn from stories.

Further, the stories that we tell tend to follow the same structure employed in novels, movies, the theatre, and even your favorite opera (ours is *Candide*). The first step in crafting *your* story is to begin with your organization, your existing customers, and your competition. What is your organization's current reality—are your customers satisfied, are they loyal, in what way do they perceive your brand, what characterizes your competition? Second, based on your current state of business, what is your opportunity or challenge, your call to action, your BIG IDEA? Third, what are the challenges standing in your way to making this call to action, your big idea, a reality? And, who within, or external to, your organization can help with this? What weaknesses do you need to address before you go any further? Fourth, as you pursue this newly defined opportunity, you begin to enter uncharted territory. What is your plan to communicate this new "adventure" to your key stakeholders, namely, your employees, customers, prospective new customers, and suppliers?

Rose and Pulizzi go on and further distill this multistep process into what they call the *Story Map,* consisting of three acts; Act 1: Establishing the Hero, Act 2: Establishing the Vision, and Act 3: Victory—The New World. In terms of the content, in Act 1, the story focuses on various pain points, whether your organization's or your customers', and what your customers are putting up with or dealing with in the current state of affairs. It's in this first act that you foreshadow what *could* be or what *is* coming from your company to help your customers. In Act 2, your story focuses on how you are going to meet, or have met, your challenge—this could be a new product, a new service, a renewed emphasis and clearer positioning, or communication of a current product or service—and how you're ready to challenge the status quo. Act 3 is where and how, including social media, you publicize how you've met the challenge and succeeded in making your customers' lives, in some way, better.

Action Step #2

Put on your screenplay writer's hat and create your organization's story map, its three-act performance. Who or what is your hero? Is it a new product or service, a new process, a renewed focus on customer service, or is it your new director of engineering? How will your hero win over your customers with your efforts and in what way are you really challenging your industry's status quo? Finally, in Act 3, how are you going to communicate your heroic accomplishments via social media?

Liquid and Linked

As we're hoping you've experienced thus far, all the three acts within the story map provide magnificent content with which to evolve a compelling company or brand story. Add to this the fact that online social media, ever since Facebook began as a way for college students to tell their "story," has fast become a prominent stage for brands to tell their own story, and that the process by which brands develop and communicate their unique story becomes highly liquid and highly linked.[6] *Liquid* in that brand stories fueled by social media are fluid, sharable, and ever evolving. *Linked* in that brand stories and the chapters within those stories are now connected across multiple online and social platforms (e.g., your website, Facebook, Twitter, Instagram). So, unlike the ubiquitous 30-second TV commercial that simply delivers a monologue and tells a one-way story, storytelling fueled by social media becomes dynamic and connected storytelling, where the brand hero's journey and story occurs over time and across myriad online social platforms.

Social Fire Starters

In this chapter, we've gone over the importance of crafting stories and the act of storytelling toward building your brand, company, or organization narrative and story map via social media. A recent article published on the website Social Media Today[7] outlined several ways that brands can turn uninspired company content into content that tells the story of who you are and what you stand for. Five social fire starters highlighted in the article include:

1. Create a character
2. Integrate your brand's values
3. Take people behind the scenes
4. Recount your origins
5. Employ metaphors and comparisons

Let's examine each of the five fire starters in detail.

Creating a Character

In 2008, the automotive insurance company Progressive created a quirky, upbeat and, to some, annoying brand character and mascot named Flo to help the company put forth a friendly persona. As stated in *AdAge*, "Consumers would rather interact with a cute or cuddly character than with a faceless corporate executive." In terms of Flo's effect on Progressive's ability to reach and engage with consumers, it's interesting to note that toward late 2013, Progressive's Facebook page had generated just over 160,000 likes whereas Flo's page had over 5,000,000 likes! "Like" her or not, Flo's Facebook, Twitter presence (20,000+ followers), and YouTube presence (Progressive has a YouTube channel with almost 7,000 subscribers featuring Flo, with several videos generating over 1 million views each) has generated significant impressions and engagement among consumers.

In linking Flo's character with Progressive's recent revenue and profit growth, Progressive CMO Jeff Charney states that the brand's efforts with Flo helped in part to deliver the insurance company's positive results "by out-creating the competition, not outspending them."[8] Compared to the boring, uninspiring, and commodity-like insurance brands that we have grown used to, the Flo character and ongoing narrative helped Progressive forge an emotional connection where prior none had existed.

However, brands beware; although your mascot may never run afoul of the law (see Dell and its infamous intern[9]) or engage in immoral behavior, the person representing your brand, or as in Progressive's case, the brand persona herself, may become attached to controversy simply because of its social media presence. This is where your storytelling needs to stop and where your corporate response needs to take over.

This occurred with Progressive in 2012 when it tweeted on its main Twitter account (with a smiling Flo as its Twitter picture) a series of canned responses regarding the tragic death of a Progressive customer in a car accident. Now, it doesn't take a PhD in Social Media Marketing to wonder why Progressive didn't replace Flo's *avatar* with its corporate logo on its Twitter account as it dealt in court with subsequent claims related to the accident. So, Flo (the character and persona) sadly became linked to Progressive's unfortunate and unwise handling of its social media responses and become the target of numerous emails slamming both her as well as Progressive. Lesson learned? Don't mistake the cute and cuddly characters you may create to represent your company as actual company representatives when the context moves beyond branding, advertising, and storytelling.

Integrating Your Brand's Values

Another social fire starter is to reflect on your brand's values and what you stand for as a company and to apply this as an element of your brand's social media narrative and presence. From The Body Shop and its focus on ethics and integrity in selling cosmetics, to (PRODUCT) RED and its partnership with brands such as Apple, Beats, and Starbucks to fund AIDS or HIV programs, to the ice cream brand Ben & Jerry's, brand stories that move beyond purely functional or even benefit-driven appeals to higher level brand associations help foster more engaging and meaningful content. As much as we like facts and features, we love and even crave stories and the narratives that weave those facts and features within the fabric of the story.

Taking Us Behind the Scenes

Consider a third social fire starter: taking your customer behind the scenes. The online retailer Zappos does a magnificent job of allowing us, the prospective shoe buyer, to peek behind the scenes at one of the most lauded retailers in terms of its ability to deliver outstanding customer service. Zappos' story originates with its founder, Tony Shei, and his passion for taking care of Zappos' customers as well as its employees. For instance, Zappos has a YouTube channel that provides the company a platform for showcasing its employees' dedication to servicing its customers. Many of these YouTube videos literally go behind the scenes into the Zappos' office space, showing the energy and camaraderie that takes place among Zappos' employees.

Taking people behind the scenes can also mean creating a level of transparency and confronting issues head on. This happened several years ago when two employees at a Domino's Pizza franchise in North Carolina created a video of themselves doing disgusting things to the food they were supposedly serving up to unsuspecting customers and posted the video on YouTube. Within twenty-four hours, the Domino's CEO was featured in his own YouTube video responding to the initial video, defending the company and its thousands of franchisees and conveying the seriousness with which Domino's viewed the incident. Instead of hoping and praying the incident and video would be forgotten or issuing a standard press release defending the company, Domino's figuratively brought us into the boardroom to hear the "guy in charge" respond and take action.

Recounting Your Origins

A fourth approach to fueling your brand story is to recount your origins and heritage as a company or organization. As successful (and big) as brands such as Apple, Starbucks, and Gatorade are, we sometimes forget that they once were actually small players in their respective markets. For instance, the sports drink Gatorade along with its agency TBWA\Chiat\Day recently developed a campaign meant to take us back to the 1960s and the University of Florida where Gatorade began as a drink concocted to fuel the Florida Gators football players in the hot and humid climes of Gainesville. Another example involves Coca-Cola and its ability to foster nostalgic feelings for the brand based on its appeal across several decades. Taken together, these types of stories help us to ascribe deeper meaning and feelings of nostalgia to brands that we (no offense) may have begun to take for granted.

Use Metaphors

The fifth story fire starter—employing metaphor and comparison—involves a tried-and-true interviewing technique called *projective questioning* designed to elicit responses that go beyond surface-level answers. For instance, if we wanted to find out what the car brand Mercedes-Benz meant to you, we could ask you just that: "When you think of Mercedes-Benz cars, what comes to mind?" And, you might respond something like, "I think they're really nice, yet they're also kind of expensive." However, what if we asked you "If you were to compare a Mercedes-Benz car to a [movie star, animal, pro athlete, etc.], which would it be and what visuals would represent the brand?" The point here is that by eliciting metaphorical comparisons, an approach pioneered and patented by Harvard Business School professor Gerald Zaltman with his Zaltman metaphor elicitation technique (ZMET) research methodology, we can generate deeper level and nonliteral meanings, insights, and thoughts (thoughts that we often find difficult to express in words) through images and projections related to how we perceive specific brands.

Combining our first fire starter (creating a character) with the use of metaphors and comparisons, an effective social narrative can also involve what we'll refer to as the "Mr. Clean" approach. In case you were born in the 1990s or later, Mr. Clean was a character created with superhuman cleaning powers or at least really strong arms. He conveyed strength, dependability, and confidence—all the things a cleaning brand can communicate in words, yet not with the same effect. Or, imagine you are founder and CEO of Joe's Termite Company. For example, perhaps you (Joe) could create a character with superpower, Justice League-type strength with which to combat those pesky, wood-eating termites and leverage this character throughout his social media presence. This could involve creating a Facebook page featuring the character; we'll call it *the Termite-inator*, its own Twitter account, a *big* presence on Joe's website—you get the picture. While we don't *really* believe that such a character *actually* exists, the meaning behind the Termite-inator is clear—he or she will help you in your (Joe's) battle for termite supremacy.

Action Step #3

Considering your organization or brand and what it stands for, which of the five social fire starters align best with your opportunities or challenges?

In short, engaging people (your customers, your employees, your children, for that matter) with stories and story narratives is a great way to connect with them. Particularly in this cluttered, messy, and complex world of online and offline media, if you can't make that connection with your respective audience(s) on a level that goes beyond mere awareness, then you risk, at best, being ignored and, at worst, being irrelevant. Again, the act of persuasion is at the heart of getting people to take action, and one proven pathway to persuasion is to engage people in story.

Once upon a time...

The Insider's Perspective
Philipp Reker, founder, The Roadery

In 2012, I left the advertising and entertainment industry in LA and began to form an idea for a business that would allow people to experience the beauty, culture, and mystique of the open road and the great American West. Having grown up in Germany and having worked in the luxury car industry for Mercedes-Benz, I've always been fascinated by the combination of finely crafted vehicles and travel. Thus was born my customized motorcycle touring company and brand called The Roadery. As a start-up, we didn't have too much money to spend on generating awareness and interest in The Roadery concept. We started with a story and narrative we thought would connect and resonate with people young and old—one focusing on the phenomenon that we are all in a hurry, all the time, and we seldom take the time to reconnect with some of the most fundamental things in life: nature, friendship, and adventure. Because of our limited advertising and promotions budget, we depended heavily on our social media presence, including our Facebook site as well as Instagram, as platforms with which to tell our story.

CHAPTER 4

Creating Your Content

When it comes to putting social media to practice, the challenge that most brands face is that they base their strategy and execution simply on which social platforms (*where*) they want to be on rather than *who* they want to engage and *what* story they want to tell. Brands establish (independent of each platform) a presence on Facebook, Instagram, and Twitter pages, start posting, and then simply wait for their audience to interact and engage with them. With no overall strategy in place, these brands dive feet first into the social media pool and start posting content on various social media platforms without any strategic considerations. And why not? That's where the action is. This is the space where we all can be creative. It's tangible—and fun to post stuff! Who needs to talk about strategy? Let's just do it!

This is what we call being *tactic happy*. Being tactic happy means someone in your marketing or PR department decides unilaterally it's a good idea to create a bunch of blog posts, videos, infographics, and e-books and post them everywhere, and then hope for some overwhelming response—significant increases in likes, shares, comments, ratings, followers, and of course, sales lift. You have a marketing budget to spend, and you expect something in return—this is called return on investment or ROI. And, ROI is what your boss or what your boss's boss uses to measure the success of your marketing initiatives. You want your social media initiatives to provide greater [fill in the blank] for the company— greater likes, shares, comments, ratings, followers, and sales. And when this doesn't happen, you (and your boss) get discouraged. We like to call this the *reality bites* moment. It's when you realize that all of the great and creative work you did amounts to very little. Why? Because you started with the *where* and not with the *who* and the *what*.

Robert Rose, chief strategist at the Content Marketing Institute, stated it perfectly, "I see the biggest mistake (brands make) is in the way that social ROI is defined. ROI is a result. It's something that happens. It is not a prerequisite to something that we do. And most marketing organizations that suffer from this have to 'prove ROI' beforehand. The edict comes down to say 'show me the ROI' before you actually go out and do it."[1] This is why you have to put a strategy in place before you create even one piece of content.

Action Step #1

Where does *your organization* currently stand with its social media presence? Now's the perfect time to perform an audit of your current social initiatives—where is your brand or organization online? Are you present in the primary social networks? (e.g., Facebook, LinkedIn, Twitter)? Don't get hung up on numbers at this point—for instance, how many followers or likes you have. Look at your engagement. How many people are commenting and sharing your content? *Who* is following you? Are these the audiences you want to engage? Are you tracking behaviors and activity (are you using Google Analytics, Facebook Insights, TweetDeck, and other measurement tools)? This is not a deep dive into analytics—you can do that later. In a nutshell, this exercise is about how your social presence is working for you.

Creating a Content Marketing Strategy

All men can see these tactics whereby I conquer, but what none can see is the strategy out of which victory is evolved.

—Sun Tzu, The Art of War

The best pathway to social media marketing success is to first create a content marketing strategy (CMS). While it may not be as tangible (or exciting) as creating the content, a CMS provides you a roadmap, sets your path, and keeps you focused on six key elements:

1. Why
2. Who
3. What
4. How

5. Where

6. Did it work?

We talked about the *why* in the first chapter. In this chapter, we focus on the *who* (who do you want to and need to engage), the *what* (what story do you want to tell), and the *how* (how will you tell it). By identifying these three pillars of your strategy, you're one step closer to creating a solid foundation upon which to execute your social media plan and to deliver on the ever-important ROI.

Who Do You Want to Engage?

In Chapter 1, you worked to define your *why*. Now, it's time to define your customers. When we think of our audience(s) as an amalgam of demographics and statistics, we call them consumers. When we go deeper and begin to understand what actually drives them, how they relate to our brand, and what makes them tick, we think of them as people. This is a critical differentiation that will influence how you move forward with all of your marketing initiatives. When we are able to accept our audiences as real people, we make it more real, personal, and relevant.

At the end of the day, we are all consumers of products and services. It doesn't matter if your audience is stay-at-home moms (SAHMs), double income, no kids (DINKs), or the ever-popular *My Baby Is Cuter Than Your Baby* (MBICTYB) segment; properly defined segments all tend to have unique characteristics and expectations. For instance, when a company chooses to launch an e-commerce solution, they usually start with "what does Amazon do?" When you shop online, don't you often find yourself saying, "I wish this site worked more like Amazon's." Why is that? Because Amazon sets the standard, and your customers are the same. They have specific expectations when it comes to how they want to interact with your brand.

Your job is to understand first *who* they are and what motivates them. In doing so, there are three things you will want to identify about your audiences:

1. What are their pain points? What bothers them? What are they putting up with? What problems are they facing with or without your brand?

2. How they spend their day? Do they go to work? Do they use public transportation or do they drive? Do they travel? Are they always on the go? Do they suffer from the FOMO (fear of missing out) syndrome? How do they spend their downtime?

3. How do they consume content? Do they use their phones? Do they prefer a tablet to a laptop? Do they listen to podcasts? Do they print out PDFs to read later?

Here's a mini case study to illustrate the importance of the *who*: Marcus Sheridan, also known as the *Sales Lion*, was the CEO of River Pools and Spas, a fiberglass pool company in Virginia. In 2007, River Pools and Spas was the market share laggard in its market. It was generating $4.5 million in sales and spending $250,000 in traditional marketing annually. Flash forward to 2010 when River Pools and Spas began to sell more fiberglass pools than any other pool retailer in North America—yet it only spent $40,000 in marketing to do so.

How did the Sales Lion and his team do this? *Content marketing.* Marcus started a blog. He uncovered *who* his customers were and what kinds of questions they had about pools and all things related to pools. He then wrote a blog post for every single question and created the *Most Educational Swimming Pool Blog in the Country!* —yes, that was the title of his blog. Marcus learned that his customers were using Google to conduct research and had a lot of questions. So he created content and put it where they were. He knew *who* they were and what they wanted.

Action Step #2

Sit back and think about what customers you really want to, or need to, engage. Do you really understand who they are or are they simply a bunch of statistics and demographics? Let's create a simple persona. For example, let's say you work for a company that sells customizable products made from personal photographs, and your primary audience is SAHMs. Let's call one of those moms Joanne. Who is she? How does she live? How does she spend her time? What does she love? What are her pain points? How does she consume content? How does she feel about her kids?

Joanne

- Thirty, married, two kids (five and eight).
- A SAHM.
- Parent–teacher association (PTA) and room mother.
- Lives on her Apple 5S—in fact, she lost it once and freaked out!
- Joanne's friends look to her for trends and fashion advice.
- Joanne loves her home. She is always decorating and changing things around.
- She is proud of her things and her family and likes to show them off.
- She is a do-it-yourself (DIY) kind of person. She used to make her kids' Halloween costumes.
- She wants to scrapbook more.
- She is always looking for fun things to do with the family—hikes, day trips, museums, and vacations.
- Of course, Joanne is pressed for time.
- Between shuttling the kids around, coffees and lunches with friends, spinning and yoga, cooking and shopping, she has very little time to research products and read or learn about them, online and offline. Her content needs to be viewed while she waits in line at carpool or at soccer practice.
- She loves fashion and entertainment. She still buys *People*, *Vanity Fair*, and *US Weekly* at the checkout counter.
- However, she's fast becoming 100 percent digital. She spends the little free time she has on the following platforms: Facebook, Pinterest, Fab (a mobile shopping app), and Instagram.

This is the type of personal-level detail you should be thinking about when getting to know and describing the valued customers that make up your audience.

What Do You Want to Say?

As we've argued previously, storytelling has been around since the dawn of time, and it's how human beings have been relating to one another century after century. It's in our DNA. And, having read the last chapter, you know that the best way to engage your audience is through story. However, your story must be a story that resonates with your "Joanne"— it must offer a narrative that grabs her attention and pulls her into your brand experience. In fact, *your* story becomes *her* story. It's no longer about you and your brand—it is about your audience and their wishes, wants, and needs. Peter Guber, a seasoned Hollywood producer and storyteller, argues that "stories are a misunderstood, misused, and underutilized asset, and if I could shine a light on them and identify a process, it would be a tremendous benefit. I spent all these years doing stories and now the story is the story. Stories aren't the icing on the cake; they are the cake!"[2]

The challenge that companies of all shapes and sizes face is that the marketplace is noisy, and therefore brands continue to battle to differentiate themselves and rise above the clutter. And, the more they battle, the worse the clutter becomes. You've heard of industry research stating that people (you and I and Joanne) are bombarded by thousands of marketing messages every day. That's a lot of noise! So how does your company or brand stick out in the crowd? How do you engage members of your audience who are sick and tired of being "targeted" with ads and promotions? Through compelling stories and your ability to weave your story's narrative across traditional, digital, and social media channels. One visual that helps us is to think of your story as a quilt and your narratives told across the various media as the squares that make up your quilt. In short, it may be easier to simply publish a bunch of content, yet that doesn't mean that anyone will listen or take notice.

Joe Pulizzi, founder of the Content Marketing Institute, proposes that "brands have been telling stories to attract and retain customers for hundreds of years. The difference today is that the barriers to entry (content acceptance, talent and technology) no longer exist for brands to get into the publishing arena."[3] All it takes is a Facebook page or a WordPress site, and you too can publish within seconds. But that does not ensure engagement. Let us repeat—simply creating a Facebook page or a blog does not ensure engagement!

Action Step #3

Reflect back to your action step in Chapter 3 where you played screenplay writer, identified your brand or company "hero," and also identified some social fire starters. Now, begin to craft your brand's story. Note that this is not your mission statement. You know *who* you want to engage. Your story should be based on *what* you want to say to them that will inspire them to take action—and that action could be as simple as signing up for an e-mail or buying your product.

How Do You Want to Say It?

Now that you know *who* you want to engage and *what* you want to tell them, you can decide *how* you want to tell it. Remember that one of the reasons we create personas such as Joanne's is to understand *how* your audiences consume content. So this should be easy, right? Well, not really. Beware; just because now you understand your audience's content consumption habits better doesn't mean you'll necessarily hold back on throwing content against the wall, hoping some of it will stick. The fact is that too many brands (small, medium, and big brands managed by smart MBAs) still get carried away and create way too much content and manage way too many platforms.

Recent research shows that most business-to-business (B2B) and business-to-consumer (B2C) companies are managing up to 12 different tactics at any given time, where these tactics range from blog postings, social media posts, articles and white papers, videos, in-person events, e-books, and more. At first, this sounds really exciting—360-degree marketing in action! Yet, it can be difficult, regardless of company size, to maintain a consistent brand message across so many tactics. This is where you need to be careful and not bite off more than you can chew. We suggest choosing your initial tactics based on two filters:

1. *Internal skills*: What kinds of content can your internal team produce? Do you have writers? Videographers? Designers?
2. *Audience engagement*: What story or narrative will resonate with your audience? What forms of content and which media, or content channels, will help you reach and engage them?

The initial tactics you choose will more than likely be a mix of traditional, digital, and social media and marketing initiatives. Similar to the paid, owned, and earned media framework (POEM) we discussed in Chapter 1, the goal is to focus on spreading your reach and narrative across paid, owned, and earned content types.

Paid Content

Paid content is exactly as it sounds; it's where you pay for placement. It involves traditional media such as television, radio, and print ads as well as digital banner ads and keyword buys through paid search platforms such as Google AdWords. It has also been called *interruptive marketing* because of its invasive nature. Others call it *spray and pray*: "You spray money on 'unaccountable' media and pray for results." However, when you spray cockroaches, they ultimately become immune to the effects of the spray. In a way, we're all like cockroaches—the more and more we get sprayed by advertising, the less effective it is. So, whereas paid media and content remains important because of its ability to buy reach, it is expensive (note the continually increasing ad rates for 30-second Super Bowl spots), and smaller brands often do not have the budget for it.

Owned Content

Owned content is simply that—it's content that you create and own. It's the core of your CMS, and includes your website, your company blog, or your Facebook presence. Owned content also includes the content you create for your paid media—you just distribute it at no incremental cost on platforms such as YouTube and Vimeo. For example, brands often create amazing (and expensive) commercials that are aired on paid media (e.g., television), yet are also shown on their own websites and other online channels such as YouTube.

This is what the car brand Volkswagen (VW) and its agency Deutsch did when it prereleased its commercial featuring a little Darth Vader titled "The Force" prior to its airing during the 2012 Super Bowl. Before the two teams even kicked off on national television, the commercial had been viewed over 20 million times via "free" media on platforms such as YouTube. They took paid content and made it owned content. They extended the life of The Force commercial by placing it online where it continues to get millions upon millions of views as we write. If the commercial had come out 10 years earlier, it would have aired on Super Bowl Sunday and perhaps for a few weeks after, but that would have been it. By turning paid media into owned content, the commercial, and the cute little Darth Vader starring in it, lives on.

Earned Content

Earned content is the brass ring of marketing. This is when all of your efforts pay off because other people, brands, and news outlets are talking about and sharing the content you have created. It's what every brand should hope and strive for—you've created a piece of content so good that AdWeek, CNN, and Mashable are all talking about it. It happened to VW when The Force commercial became a news item in itself and was covered by the business and popular press. It happened with the brand Reebok when it introduced its Terry Tate "Office Linebacker" character during the 2003 Super Bowl. And it happened when Old Spice launched its Old Spice Guy campaign that generated over 40 million views in one week on YouTube with 1.4 billion free media impressions.

Yet, you do not have to be a well-known brand spending millions of dollars to create paid content that becomes earned content. Sprinkles Cupcakes opened its first store in Beverly Hills in 2005. By March of 2011, they were opening their tenth store in New York City (NYC). Their agency, Bullfrog & Baum, launched a two-week campaign delivering cupcakes to key media contacts all over NYC. Each box had a sticker with the @Sprinkles Twitter handle and Facebook address. Within two weeks, they increased their Twitter followers by almost 4,000. But more importantly, they garnered earned media all over the place: *People Magazine*, Bravo, CNN (Anderson Cooper), *Allure, New York Daily News,* and *InStyle*. On the NYC store's opening day, people waited in line for more than 30 minutes just to buy a cupcake. It worked!

Action Step #4

Do you have any earned content? Sure you do! Search for your brand on Google—what comes up? Is it positive? Is it being shared? If so, good job.

If you don't find much, create some content along the lines of little Darth Vader, Terry Tate, or Old Spice's Mustafa—and as with the Sprinkles case, it doesn't have to be a million-dollar production. And, it can put you on the map, at least the social media map.

The Insider's Perspective

Robert Rose, chief strategist, Content Marketing Institute

As the growth of the social and mobile Web continues, there's little doubt that the relationships between business and consumer have fundamentally transformed. The biggest challenge is that most businesses have not. As consumers publish and share their opinions (good and bad) with increasing ease, they risk becoming more persuasive than even the company's voice itself—one that still operates from the blind eye of "command and control" communication models.

It's up to us as marketers to create, lead, and build loyalty among our different consumer groups so that they work optimally for our business. At the heart of this leadership and loyalty strategy is one thing—*content marketing*. To succeed today, we need to leverage content to continually engage our audiences—from the first time we meet them, continuing on throughout the entire customer lifecycle. In short, the job of marketing is no longer to create customers. It is (to paraphrase Peter Drucker) to create passionate, loyal subscribers and ambassadors to our brand.

CHAPTER 5

If Content Is King, Then Distribution Is Queen

How to Manage Your Story Across Social Media

We previously argued that most brands risk failing with their social media strategy because they start with the *where* first—they adopt a platform-centric strategy rather than first defining with whom they want to engage and with what type of content. Well, now that you have identified the *who* (who you want to engage), the *what* (what you want to tell them), and the *how* from Chapter 4, now's the time to focus on the *where*—those digital and social platforms that make most strategic sense for your specific situation, brand, or organization.

Yet be forewarned; this is not a simple exercise. You're not just simply setting up a Facebook page or a Twitter account and executing a few posts every week. The process of telling your story across digital and social media takes a lot of planning as well as effort to monitor, manage, and measure the effectiveness of your social storytelling. In other words, this takes a good deal of time. However, before we dive into the three Ms of social media content (manage, monitor, and measure), we need to look back at where we've been thus far.

How and Where Does Your Audience Consume Content?

By this point in your strategy development, you have a good idea as to who you want to engage—your audience. You've developed your consumer personas and you know what makes them tick. At the same time, you understand how they consume content. Do they consume content using their smartphones or tablets or laptops or now what we call "phablets," the merging of the phone and tablet? Where smartphones are great for consuming content on the go or while waiting in line at Whole Foods, tablets are great for cuddling up to your favorite book or movie, and laptops are for—well—work. Does your audience prefer long-form content types such as videos, white papers, and blogs, or quick bits of content such as pictures, short Vine-type videos, or infographics?

It's critical to understand this because it influences not only what content tactics you employ but also what kind of talent and skillsets you need to create the content. This leads to a larger discussion of scope, schedule, and budget and leads to the question, "Do we do this in-house or do we hire an agency?" More on that later in this chapter; let's not get ahead of ourselves.

Next, you need to know where your audience is consuming their content—because this is where you need to be too. So where are they? Are they on Facebook? Pinterest? LinkedIn? Instagram? And please don't say your closest competitor's website. Sure, your audience is probably checking out your competition, but that shouldn't concern you as much as another form of competition. Why? Because not only are you competing with other firms in your industry but more importantly you're competing for share of mind, share of conversation, and share of attention. Your competition is actually the latest fad, trend, meme, social media platform, app, viral video, and mobile game. To get you to read this chapter on that flight from Atlanta to Dallas, we the authors are currently competing with content such as Robin Thicke's "Blurred Lines," *Angry Birds Star Wars*, *Flappy Bird*, the final season of *Breaking Bad*, *Clash of Clans*, *Temple Run*, and many, many more! This is where you could be right now—yet you're reading this book.

So, how are you going to compete? How are you going to grab and command your audience's attention and engage? It takes not only compelling, creative content but planning as well.

Editorial Calendar—the Planning Process

One of the keys to a successful social media marketing strategy is the *content editorial calendar*, because it allows you to plan ahead and create a schedule that clearly outlines what you are saying, how you are saying it, and where you are going to say it. There are a number of ways you can approach this. First, you can simply create what we like to call a *velocity schedule*, as shown in the following table. This type of schedule simply states how many posts per month will take place for each platform. For instance, the example shows that the content team will be creating 4 blog posts in August and 8 more in December, while posting on Facebook 16 times each month. The idea here is to plan for velocity—how much content will need to be created each month—where the research, preproduction, and production windows allow for the creation of that content.

A Velocity Schedule

Platform	June	July	August	September	October	November	December
Blog	Research		4	4	8	8	8
YouTube	Preproduction		Production	2	4	4	4
e-Books	Preproduction		Production	2	2	2	2
Instagram	8	8	12	12	16	20	20
Facebook	16	16	16	16	16	16	16
Pinterest	Research	8	8	8	8	8	8

Or, you can get much more detailed with this second example that follows. In the following editorial calendar, you plan each post or piece of content by a specific date and by the specific social platform; you also plan what tags are to be embedded, who is going to create it, and what assets you will need. This kind of calendar allows you to plan ahead while assigning responsibility and creating accountability.[1]

The Three Ms: Manage, Monitor, and Measure

Without making the effort to manage, monitor, and measure your content, you risk driving down the social media highway with no road map and no guardrails for those treacherous stretches where things become really, really complex. If so, you might just as well put the book down right now and finish watching that last season of *Breaking Bad*. Although this may seem harsh, it's the truth. If your content marketing and social strategy is indeed alive with daily (if not hourly) audience engagement and with your audience conversing with you, recommending you,

An Editorial Calendar

Date	Venue	Tactic	Category	Author	Topic/title	Assets
1-April	Blog	Case study: client X	Direct marketing	John	How we helped client X gain 100,000 users	Copy, screenshots, graphs
1-April	Twitter	Broadcast case study: client X	Broadcast	Shawn	Check out our latest case study on client X	Link
1-April	Facebook	Post case study: client X	Broadcast/support	Shawn	Check out our latest case study on client X	Thumbnail, link
3-April	Blog	How to #5	CRM	Susan G	How to gain more customers and e-mail them	Copy
3-April	Twitter	Broadcast how to #5	Broadcast	Shawn	Want to learn how to get more customers and e-mail them?	Link
3-April	Facebook	Post how to #5	Broadcast/support	Shawn	Want to learn how to get more customers and e-mail them?	Thumbnail, link
5-April	Slideshare	CEO presentation at CMW	Presentation	Susan C	Agency's keynote at CMW 2013	PDF
5-April	Twitter	Broadcast CEO presentation	Broadcast	Shawn	See our CEO's keynote at CMW 2013	Link
5-April	Facebook	Post CEO presentation	Broadcast/support	Shawn	See our CEO's keynote at CMW 2013	Thumbnail, link

Abbreviations: CRM, Customer relationship management; CMW, Content Marketing World conference.

complaining to you, clicking through to you, and quite possibly ordering and buying from you, how else can you effectively execute your strategy without managing, monitoring, and measure your success (or failure)?

The Manage Step

Managing your content means sticking to your editorial calendar, delegating tasks to copywriters, designers, and developers (if you're fortunate enough to have these resources) and choosing which content tactics to employ. With multiple personas with differing needs potentially making up your audience, you'll be busy creating and publishing content on a daily basis. As the Content Marketing Institute's Robert Rose and Joe Pulizzi state, "The job of marketing is no longer to create customers, it is to create passionate subscribers to our brand." To achieve this, you need to be on top of managing your content every single day and this is where a disciplined approach to developing and updating an editorial calendar helps.

#Hashtags

Another important, and often misunderstood, way to manage your social media content is through the use of the ubiquitous #. A recent post on Social Media Today called the use of hashtags on Twitter, Instagram, and now Facebook the social media equivalent to search engine optimization (SEO) and search engines. Simply put, a well-thought-out hashtag strategy will enable you to categorize your content by themes or categories or other keywords and allow interested and engaged individuals (your customers or prospects) to find your content more easily. Whether your hashtags are directly tied to your brand, your story and narrative, your product, or other categories, make sure they're relevant! For instance, one of our favorite old-school rockers, Iggy Pop, accentuates his already strong social media presence (almost 1.2 million Facebook likes and 20,000 Twitter followers) with hashtags such as #iggypop and #lustforlife that enable his fan base to efficiently locate and aggregate content about him.

The #one #caveat #with #the #use #of #hashtags? Less is more...try to limit your hashtag use to three or less per post. If not, you risk—well, you get it.

The Monitor Step

In the old days, *way back* to the 1980s and 1990s, when you published content, it was literally a one-way street, a monologue, a lecture. It was difficult if not impossible for your audience to comment, discuss, share, or rate you on a large scale. Even an article or banner ad published online worked from the same dynamic as a radio or television commercial. You put it out there and hoped people would notice or read it. Today, the objective is that your customers will not only read, watch, or attend to your content, but that they will also engage, converse, comment, and share. This requires your organization to monitor *all* activity on *all* of your social and digital platforms. And not just to listen but to respond as well and proactively start or continue the discussion. You should also consider putting into place some form of social media governance guidelines to protect your brand's integrity and to create guardrails for those of you representing your brand or organization online. But more on that later in this chapter.

There are myriad monitoring platforms and tools (e.g., Integrasco, Brandtology, Percolate, HootSuite) that help organizations monitor their digital and social initiatives as well as listen to the chatter related to the brand or organization; some are free and some can be quite expensive. Platforms such as HootSuite are accessible to small organizations with affordable monthly rates. Google Alerts and TweetDeck are great tools that are free and literally take minutes to download or set up. With Google Alerts, you make a few selections, choose some keywords, and your inbox begins to fill up with alerts and information.

Monitor the Web for Interesting New Content

Google Alerts are email updates of the latest relevant Google results (Web, news, etc.) based on your queries.

Enter a search query you wish to monitor. You will see a preview of the type of results you'll receive. Some handy uses of Google Alerts include:

- Monitoring a developing news story
- Keeping current on a competitor or industry

- Getting the latest on a celebrity or event
- Keeping tabs on your favorite sports teams

With TweetDeck, you schedule tweets to be sent immediately or delivered later, and you can also set up a series of custom columns that display your Twitter activity.

The Measure Step

As stated earlier, if you are not willing or able to measure the performance of your social content, then (as in the Talking Heads' song) you risk traveling on the road to nowhere. Measurement can be very simple and yet it can also be extremely complicated. It really comes down to the goals you set and how you measure your performance against those goals. For instance, your goal may be to get more Facebook likes, shares, comments, or posts, or Twitter followers. These are quite simple metrics that you can measure with Facebook Insights or TweetDeck. You create and publish content and see if your metrics rise or fall over time. Simple, and fun!

For example, let's say you're the community manager for Wooly Socks, a company that creates and sells fancy wool socks. You set up a Facebook page and a YouTube channel. You use Facebook to post fun stories and facts about your socks and you use YouTube to broadcast interesting videos on the history of socks, factory tours, and your sock-making process. You also use Facebook to broadcast your videos.

The goal of all this content is to educate, engage your customer, and lead them to your e-commerce enabled website. This is where the Google Analytics platform comes in. Through the use of Google Analytics, you can measure what online sites your customers came from, what web pages they viewed and how long they stayed on these pages, their bounce rate (meaning what percentage of woolysocks.com visitors came and left after only one page visit), what keywords they used in search engines, and where and when they either bought or abandoned their shopping cart. In addition to Facebook Insights, YouTube also offers analytic tools to help you measure how many people are engaging with your content, how often they share it, and the volume of comments.

The idea here is to show you that there are lots of tools (and many of these tools are free) to measure your activity within your social and digital ecosystem. By first establishing your goals, you can measure which content is resonating to help you gain insights on ways to foster even greater customer engagement as well as identify which content you need to revise or improve.

Organizing for Social Media

Through social media platforms such as Facebook, Twitter, Instagram, Pinterest, and many others, your company, your organization, your brand is now (more than ever) present on what we call *the front line*, whether you like it or not. The one question we get asked repeatedly is, "How do we organize internally for the new front line?" In other words, it's one thing to talk about the concept, yet it's a totally different thing to align your internal resources toward it.

Start with the chief content officer (CCO). This is the person who develops and owns your overall digital and social content strategy. He or she is the one who is accountable for its success. Please do not outsource this position. Thank you.

Next, dedicate someone in your organization to be your chief listening officer (CLO). As we will discuss in Chapter 6 related to measurement, analytics, and key performance indicators (KPIs), developing a social media content strategy does not stop at the creation stage. Remember, it lives and breathes online and within social platforms. This is the person in your organization who listens into and monitors the social activity related to your company and brand. Ideally, this is also the *rocket scientist* who is responsible for analytics, for making sense of the activity. This could be your community manager if you already have one. Or, it could be some young, social media-savvy twenty something who knows how to navigate across social platforms, who totally gets the social media ecosystem concept, and who loves numbers. Unlike your CCO, this position might also be effectively outsourced to someone outside your organization who has the necessary skillsets and who understands your organization and its social media content strategy.

Depending on the size of your organization and its resources, you will also want to dedicate someone (or a team of people) to create, produce, and manage your content across your social channels. We'll refer to this position as the managing editor(s). You might view this person or the team as similar to writers and editors in a newsroom. They are the ones with an intimate knowledge of your social channels (e.g., Facebook, Twitter, Instagram, Vine), and they take ownership of the process of strategically creating, producing, and managing your content. In a tiered organizational setting, this person or team would report to your CCO. And, as with the CCO, please do not outsource this position; it's the lifeblood of your social presence.

If your content strategy involves the creation of video, infographics, and other content that involves heavy lifting such as white papers, case studies, and testimonials, or even in-platform social games, you'll need to devote resources to managing the creation of this content with respect to scope, budgeting, and scheduling. Because your CCO and managing editor have already crafted and communicated your higher level social media marketing and content strategy so effectively, this person or people (we'll call them project managers) could be full-time, part-time, or outsourced.

Working hand in hand with your project manager will be a team of content creators and subject matter experts. The content creators are the creative people within or outside your organization (oftentimes outsourced) skilled in graphics design, video creation, or writing. They're the tacticians who bring your content strategy to life. The subject matter experts represent your company, its knowledge base, its history, its mission, and its vision. Therefore, they play a major role in the relevancy and effectiveness of your content. They can come from anywhere within your organization—your sales team, your customer service team, your engineering team, or R&D team. And, as with some of the other roles we've previously identified, this position is best kept in-house.

Taken together, the CCO, CLO, the editorial and project management functions, content creators, and your subject matter experts are aligned with your content and the story or stories driving your *why*. Depending on the size of your organization, one person might be responsible for all of the aforementioned positions. The important point is that these functions are critical to developing, executing, and maintaining an effective social media marketing strategy.

As you develop your social content, be aware that there are several important steps identified in the content production process to consider prior to your content going live. First, based on your *why* and your overall objectives, what is the theme behind the content and how will its effectiveness (your KPIs) be measured over time? Second, what type of content will you deploy and through which social channels will you communicate and spread it—is it in the form of Facebook postings, contests and prizes, Instagram photos, Vine videos, a YouTube channel, a Tumblr blog, or an active Twitter feed? Third, who will create the content, and finally, what is the process for approving this content before it goes live?

Before any piece of content is launched two procedures MUST take place:
1. Submission of the Creative Blueprint to the Digital Strategy Team
2. A Content Owner (Managing Editor) will be assigned and accountable for the lifecycle of the content type

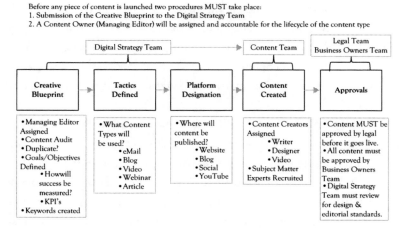

Content production process—before launch

As with the prelaunch content production process, after your content becomes live on your various social platforms, you'll need to apply what you learn from Chapter 6 (analytics and KPIs) to monitor, measure, and revise your content as necessary and determine to what extent it is supporting your objectives. The postlaunch process begins with an analytics report (this can be daily, weekly, monthly, or all three) to guide the subsequent monitoring, maintenance, and green light or red light steps.

All content published will be tracked and measured. These steps are put into place to manage and curate your content.

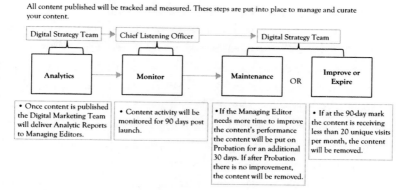

Content production process—post launch

Digital Governance

As soon as you make your first social post, you've opened the door to customer engagement, and the conversation has begun. The horses have left the chute. If you think about it, at this stage, you're giving your customers *carte blanche* to say anything they want; and when we say anything—we mean *anything*. So how are you going to deal with comments, replies, and posts that could be construed as negative or damaging to the brand? And on the other hand, how are you going to respond to comments that are positive? It's pretty simple if you think about it. You have to have a strategy, a course of action that protects the brand and at the same time establishes an action plan that includes people and procedures. This is what we call *digital governance*.

Many people confuse digital governance with how an organization builds a website or manages its content. While these functions are important, digital governance focuses on two main areas: *policies* and *standards*. For the purposes of this book, we're going to spend more time on standards than policies.

Policies are put into place to make sure the organization simply does not end up in court getting sued. These are what we call your *privacy policies* and *terms and conditions*. They protect the company and are written by senior company leadership. There are very few policies, and they do not change all that often.

Standards are very different. They aren't full of legalese. They aren't written to cover the organization's butt, should someone want to sue the company. Standards are written by subject matter experts and the people in the trenches doing the actual work. Standards are the rules that the organization follows to create a consistent digital experience, both internally and externally. They're put in place to manage the quality of the digital experience—from the look and feel of your website and your content to how you, as an organization, will interact and engage with your customers. Your standards will affect everyone in the organization who works in the digital arena and interacts with customers—every single employee. Unlike your policies, there are lots of standards and they change often.

There are several books, e-books, blogs, and white papers written on digital governance, so we won't attempt to fully explain or define it here. However, we do suggest you spend time on Lisa Welchman's website (see welchmanpierpoint.com) to understand better what she calls *web governance*.

What *is* important about digital governance, and more specifically, standards, is that it forces the organization to follow rules—or better yet, intentions—when it comes to social media engagement. Bluntly speaking, it's not a matter of *if* something goes "wrong" on one of your social channels, it's a matter of *when*. It's going to happen, and you need to be prepared. Who deals with it? How do you deal with it? Do you delete a post? Do you answer it? When do you escalate it to a more senior person on the team? These are really important questions to ask yourself and your organization.

To help you with your digital governance, we've devised a framework we like to call the *engagement alert response system* (EARS). Indeed, it sounds like something the National Security Agency would develop to monitor allies and enemies around the world, yet it's much simpler and easy to execute without hiring Massachusetts Institute of Technology's (MIT's) most talented mathematics graduates.

EARS monitors social activity and sentiment related to your brand or organization in terms of three classes: positive, negative, or indifferent. This is where your CLO translates the activity and involves other departments or parts of the company to take action where necessary. Outer ear and middle ear activity could involve a dissatisfied or disgruntled customer's posts on your Facebook followed by you alerting your customer service team; or it could involve a glowing testimonial from one of your customers that then could lead to capturing that testimonial in some content form (perhaps a short video) and communicating it across your social media ecosystem, including your website.

The purpose of EARS is to first identify if the social media "sound" or "chatter" that you're experiencing and listening to is good or bad, then to identify how the organization will "translate" the sound and to whom to send the message, and finally, applying your internal policies and standards—how your organization will deal with it.

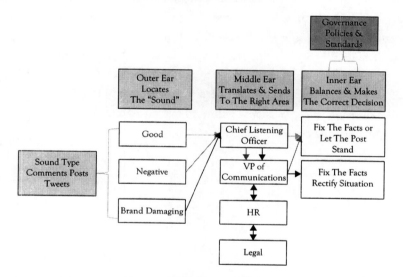

Engagement Alert Response System (EARS)

One key takeaway from this is that the boundaries separating our personal and professional lives are becoming blurred. And oftentimes we react to social posts from a personal point of view rather than a professional one. By having a digital governance approach in place and following a framework similar to our EARS, you force yourself to take a step back, look at the policies and procedures in place, and ultimately take actions that are in the best interest of your organization.

The Insider's Perspective

Jeff Wisot, vice president, Digital Enterprise Marketing, The Guitar Center Inc.

The success of a social media program is highly reliant on the foundation from which your original fan base was built. Guitar Center Enterprise has earned over 1.8 million "likes" on Facebook alone by distributing organic, native, and highly germane content. Companies and brands often focus on the *quantity* of fans, yet the strategy that thrives in the long term is one that focuses on the *quality* of its fan base. Brands suffer when likes and fans are bought and not earned... doing this results in a less engaged audience and therefore lower relevancy scores, causing their posts to be buried and rarely seen. As a result of developing a highly relevant and engaged Facebook audience base, Guitar Center recently earned over 23,000 likes on Facebook and 62,000 on Instagram by simply offering live coverage of the making of our television show "Sessions" without having to spend a single dime to distribute the content.

CHAPTER 6

Social Media Analytics

CSI: Meets Advertising

Into the classroom walked three self-proclaimed "digital data nerds" from the advertising agency RPA. Our M-School students leaned back and prepared for an onslaught of numbers and spreadsheets and, yes, the dreaded application of their math skills. Yet, unlike past courses and class sessions where applying data and numbers meant an experience akin to having a root canal, our three data nerds made the process of digital analytics, the topic of the day, actually fun and, dare we say, sexy and cool. Our students leaned forward and actually found the specific class session not only interesting but exciting as well, kind of like those crime scene investigation and forensics shows on television. Hence, the title of this chapter.

When you think about it, a day in the life of modern-day customers (yours, Amazon's, J. Crew's, your competitor's) and their consumption patterns do not involve anything close to a linear path to purchase. They operate across many screens. They search Google and navigate the paid and organic search results that appear. They "like" a brand on Facebook and are thus served with related ads in and on the right side of their Facebook timeline. They see an ad appear on the landing page of their digital version of the *New York Times* and click on it. And, yes, the modern-day consumer still does end up browsing the stacks of clothes in physical stores. The point is that the customer journey is much less linear and much more complex than in years past. And this is where the beauty and sexiness of digital and social media analytics enter the equation.

Let's take a step back in time. In the 1920s, the retailing pioneer John Wanamaker, noting the challenge of determining advertising return on investment, observed that half of the money he spent on advertising was wasted—the problem was he didn't know which half. With digital and social media, we don't face that same challenge because our online activity is completely measurable. Whether we click on a banner ad, like, share, or post something about a brand on Facebook, follow a brand on Twitter, or favor a Pinterest post, the things we do with respect to our interactions with brands online are measured and tracked digitally. On the one hand, if Wanamaker were alive today, he might sleep a bit easier knowing that his marketing mix spending would be driven and informed in part by behavioral customer data. Indeed, in the book *Digital Marketing Analytics*, the authors argue that analytics and their supporting metrics should be based on "the [customer] behaviors you are looking to change, how much you want to change them, and how long it will take to potentially change them."[1] On the other hand, Wanamaker might also lie awake at night stressing out over the vast increase in customer touch points, brought on by the rapid proliferation of online, social, and mobile media. As stated by David Krajicek in his article on marketing value and ROI, "The digitization of the marketplace and the proliferation of consumer touch points have created many more opportunities to spend (money and time) on marketing, and the impact of those new channels is often unclear."[2]

What we do know is that there is a vast amount of marketing-related data, online and offline, available to companies today from, and about, their customers. Reports indicate that digital media (including social and mobile) now account for over 20 percent of overall advertising spending.[3] Google alone processes 1 petabyte (that's 10 to the 15th power) of data *each hour*. On top of this, a recent study in *Mashable* reported that one in three millennials watch more online videos than they do TV, that is, if they watch TV at all. The study reported that online videos allow them to access the content they want and when they want it, that it feels more personal, and that it allows them to share it with others. Given the flood of digital media and data we have at our fingertips, and our continued migration to online content, the challenge facing companies today is how to analyze this data. That's what this chapter is about—applying analytics to help track and measure the effectiveness of your social media marketing. To start, we define social media analytics as the *capture, analysis, and communication of data related to your desired audience and relevant to your business on owned and earned social media platforms such as Facebook, Twitter, Instagram, and Pinterest (and myriad others), and your website.*

Analytics not only helps you monitor your social data and ascribe relevance and meaning to it, it also ties directly to the importance of establishing objectives, monitoring the progress of your social efforts toward those objectives, and even helping to determine the ROI on your social media marketing efforts. As a major retailing executive recently stated, whatever your social media marketing ROI, *not* establishing a presence in social media is tantamount to a customer walking into a store and having the salespeople ignore her.

Simply put, if you're involved in your organization's social media efforts, you may be seeing the results of prospects becoming active customers based on what your other customers have posted or shared or reviewed online. You may be experiencing an increase in positive customer sentiment as a result of your presence in various social media. In the white paper titled "ROI of Social Media: Myths, Truths and How to Measure," Dr. Natalie Petouhoff argues that "the issue of justifying the business case for social media is the B-I-G question…How do you ask for a budget for people, processes, and technology?"[4] Mastering, or at least diving into, the world of social media analytics is a start.

The important first step with analytics is to define your KPIs—those milestones, based on metrics, that you define and track, and which help you monitor your progress and determine ROI. Depending on your objectives, KPIs can include lower level metrics such as likes, shares, posts, comments, retweets, followers, and repins, or they can involve higher level metrics such as product trials, volume of sales leads, test drives, customer satisfaction, purchase intent, coupon redemptions, sales lift, or repurchase behavior. Layering on your market position (are you a new entrant or an established player?) and recognizing that different customers will exist at different stages of your customer funnel (awareness, interest, engagement, purchase or repeat purchase, advocacy), some of your KPIs will be more important than others. To help categorize and make sense of the various social KPIs, our "rock star data nerds" from RPA distill the key social KPIs into three broad types: *reach* (how many people are actually viewing your content), *engagement* (how many people are engaging with your content), and *sharing* (how many people have amplified your reach and engagement by sharing your content).

Action Step #1

It's time to work on your own KPIs. First, identify and create a list of three to five of your organization's KPIs. Next, align them with specific stages of your organization's unique customer funnel. A helpful tip: If three KPIs are good, 10 KPIs are not necessarily better. It's better to identify a short list of "key" KPIs rather than a longer list of those that if measured, may not necessarily act as a direct, accurate, or relevant indicator of performance.

A three-step starting point for beginning your analytics quest is as follows: First, identify what the behaviors or actions are that you want your audience to take related to your social media presence. Second, track those behaviors and actions based on a predetermined benchmark or starting point. In other words, track the extent to which your campaign has progressed based on your initial benchmark. Third, track your progress over a specified time period.

To help in this process, here are some examples of native and third-party social media analytics platforms that provide powerful insights into your customers' social interactions with you.

Facebook Insights

Facebook Insights is a powerful and free platform that provides metrics based on your firm's Facebook presence, such as growth or decline in Page Likes, Post Reach, as well as Engagement metrics. The most basic, the Reach metric, is the total number of unique fans who have viewed one of your posts. The Page Likes metric indicates whether likes are organic or paid, where they came from (e.g., mobile, desktop), and background demographics (e.g., male, female, country and city of origin). The Post Reach metric simply indicates the number of unique people who have seen your posts and also indicates total number of likes, comments, and shares related to those posts. The Engagement metric highlights the unique number of people who have taken some action on behalf of your posts, including liking, commenting, sharing, and clicking.

Google Analytics

Google Analytics is another powerful (and free) tool with which to bridge social media activity with activity on your website. It helps determine several important behaviors related to your website activity, namely:

- The demographics and interests of your website visitors
- The recency and frequency of their visits and whether they are new or returning visitors
- The sources of your website traffic (e.g., from domains such as Facebook, Twitter, Pinterest, other websites)
- Where they travel within your website (flow visualization)

This also includes the basics, such as

- total number of visits (and unique visits) to your site over time;
- total number of pages viewed;
- average number of pages viewed;
- average time per page view;
- overall average visit length of all your visitors;
- your website's bounce rate, meaning the percentage of visitors who leave your site after only one page visit.

YouTube Analytics

As with Facebook Insights, YouTube Analytics (YTA) enables you to understand who your YouTube content viewers are from your YouTube Channel, including gender, age range, and geographic location. YTA also helps you to identify the online sources from which viewers are finding your content and the specific sources among those that are driving viewership with the highest duration of time viewed. Finally, and this is a neat one, YTA helps you to understand better how your audience interacts with your content, including likes and dislikes, favorites, comments, and sharing activity, and highlights those portions of your video that people are watching or abandoning, as well as your retention of viewers relative to other "competing" videos of similar content and length.

Start with ROI

Now that we've defined the concept of analytics and how it relates to social media, and illustrated some pretty simple yet powerful analytics platforms in Facebook Insights, Google Analytics, and YTA, let's take a step back to Mr. Wanamaker's dilemma and then fast-forward to the twenty-first century: How might you determine an ROI scenario with respect to *your* social media marketing? When attempting to determine ROI, it's first helpful to define it. Simply put, ROI is your benefits gained less your costs incurred divided by these costs:

$$(\text{Benefits in } \$ - \text{costs in } \$/\text{costs in } \$) \times 100 = \text{ROI\%}$$

Using our previous Joe's Termite Company example, imagine Joe developed and launched a three-month social media campaign employing Facebook Sponsored Posts, compelling video content that he produced and distributed on Facebook and YouTube, and a redesigned WordPress site that Joe was able to attribute to $100,000 in incremental business. Including time, effort, video development, and a $5,000 budget for a sponsored post, Joe also attributed $25,000 cost to the campaign. So, his benefit is $100,000 and his cost is $25,000. His campaign's three-month ROI would be 300 percent:

$$(\$100,000 - \$25,000/\$25,000) \times 100 = 300\% \text{ ROI}$$

Yes, you're right—things aren't always that clean and simple in the real world. Yet, if you don't have a basis, a starting point, for measuring and determining ROI, you'll never get there. It becomes more complex when you attempt to relate social media activity with higher level KPIs. In many cases, you won't be able to determine a strict cause-and-effect relationship between social media activity and results and sales performance.

However, correlation studies can help (i.e., when X increased, so did Y), and so can attitudinal studies conducted over the time period of your social media campaign. By developing and conducting a customer survey and asking questions about customer attitudes related to your company (e.g., likeability, trustworthiness, reputation, purchase intent) and by merging this data with the behavioral data captured from your customers' social media activity during a specific campaign or time period, you can begin to attribute your social media efforts to KPIs that go beyond social media activity to more downstream metrics leading to brand favorability and preference and even sales. Further, you could even add validity to your findings by capturing survey data from a control group of consumers who were not exposed to your campaign.

Action Step #2

Take your newfound ROI skills for a test drive and choose a specific social media-driven campaign or initiative within your organization and attempt to quantify the associated benefits and costs of that campaign. Then, plug these figures into your ROI equation. The challenge you'll face is identifying the costs and benefits involved, so make sure to be consistent in the assumptions you'll need to make along the way. As you begin to apply this exercise and the ROI model over time and across specific campaigns, you will begin to quantify those initiatives that performed and those that, for some reason, did not.

Develop Your Social Scorecard

Analytics is not just about identifying and capturing metrics and measuring KPIs; it's also about making sense of the data. One approach to making sense of your social media-driven metrics and KPIs is to develop a social scorecard for monitoring your social media activity and performance over time. Companies such as the Zocalo Group[5] have developed tools and frameworks for organizing and analyzing your social and digital data in ways that add deeper meaning to it and that help you track it longitudinally.

The Zocalo Group developed a concept called the *Digital Footprint Index* (DFI) to help companies and brands understand the influence of their social media efforts. The DFI segments social media metrics by three dimensions: *height, width,* and *depth. Height* metrics include those that illustrate how much your brand is being talked about online, including blog posts, videos and photos posted, and website visits. *Width* metrics are those that illustrate your level of consumer engagement, including shares, comments, likes, video views, followers, retweets, and pins. *Depth* metrics are those that indicate the depth of consumer sentiment with your brand—are the tone of comments, posts, tweets, or other elements of your "conversations" with customers positive, negative, or indifferent? By adding dimensions to your social media activity, you're then able to discern the influence on that activity in terms of reach (height), engagement (width), and sentiment (depth).

Adding on to the DFI concept, another approach to measuring your social media effectiveness over time is to develop a social scorecard. An example of a social media scorecard would include columns for metrics, item #s or activity, a social media multiplier for weighting the relative importance of each metric, and a column indicating the specific number score for each metric as well as an overall scorecard score. In the example chart in the following text, the scorecard score is 4,640. Alone, this number means little. Taken together with your scorecard scores over time (daily, weekly, or monthly) though, this number indicates the relative growth or decline in your social media performance over certain time periods.

A Social Media Scorecard

Metrics	Item #s	Social media multiplier	Total	Overall total
FB likes	1,000	.1	100	
FB comments/shares	5,000	.3	1,500	
Twitter posts	30	.1	3	
YouTube video views	10	.4	4	
Blog posts	20	.4	8	
Website visits over 1:00 (minute)	10,000	.3	3,000	
Pinterest favorites	50	.5	25	4,640

Some tips for developing your social scorecard are to choose metrics that indeed are measurable, achievable, and that are aligned with your business objectives; weight these metrics based on their perceived relative importance (assigning them weights ranging from 0 to 1.0); and ask yourself, "What metrics are we missing?" And, if there are missing metrics that you are not able to access or determine, are there proxy metrics that you could assign to these? For instance, if you are looking to include a metric associated with overall consumer engagement, you could create a measure that is a composite of several of your direct metrics such as shares, comments, and video views.

Action Step #3

Gather a group of people within your organization or company from various departments—sales, customer service, marketing, finance, HR—and begin to develop your own social media scorecard. Your first task is to identify those metrics that are measurable, achievable, and aligned with your business objectives. Second, discuss the relative importance weighting of each metric. Third, determine a reporting mechanism that will enable you to score and track your social media efforts over time.

Advanced "Listening-In" Tools

Depending on the size and scope of your firm, social media analytics and reporting get even more interesting, and more complex. Today there are several subscription- or fee-based analytics platforms such as HootSuite, Radian6, Sysomos, and Visible Technologies that help companies and enterprises not only to measure and track social media activity but also to listen in and monitor content, conversations, and sentiment related to the firm.

Although all of these platforms are unique in their own respects, they are all characterized by features such as the ability to aggregate social media across distinct platforms (e.g., Twitter, Tumblr, Instagram, Facebook), provide customizable reporting mechanisms or dashboards, help with trend and topic tracking related to your company or brand, analyze and monitor consumer sentiment (positive, negative, or indifferent) related to your brand, and track social media-fueled brand activity across specific geographic locations. These firms (e.g., Radian6, Sysomos, Visible Technologies) have also developed more complex enterprise-wide solutions that enable companies to track and correlate social media activity directly with specific campaign and sales activity. This, too, can be divided up and analyzed by specific geographic regions.

The purpose of this chapter was to introduce you to the concepts of KPIs and ROI and the process of analytics. In the next chapter, we put it all together to highlight three case studies of small, medium, and large companies and how they applied the principles explained throughout this book, including the process of identifying your unique social media-driven metrics, KPIs, and ROI.

The Insider's Perspective
Anastasia Petukhova, owner and founder, Asilda Photography

From my experience as an entrepreneur and small business owner launching my photography business, the first important step in developing an analytics plan (actually more than important, it's critical) is to set realistic expectations for what social media can achieve relative to your company's or organization's predefined KPIs. One thing that I've learned through practice is how you'll see certain behaviors by your customers or prospective customers that are unique to each platform. For instance, Facebook is a social-intensive platform and people share content in multiple formats. Instagram and Pinterest are more visually intensive, so this leads to different behaviors and expectations. Having a clear idea of the characteristics of each different platform and its potential for delivering certain results or metrics is critical.

There are a number of different social media-driven metrics such as likes, shares and comments that may ultimately drive intermediate funnel metrics like website traffic, but it's tough to say in what way social metrics such as these relate directly to sales and other end-of-funnel metrics. So, I always remind myself to clearly define my objectives first and then measure what I can measure related to social activity. As you've highlighted in this chapter, there are lots of really effective social and online analytics platforms that are accessible to businesses of all sizes...and many are free!

It's also important to distinguish between some of the more commercial platforms (those that can actually directly drive sales) such as Instagram and Pinterest and those that are purely social in nature such as Facebook. Taking this one step further, these social platforms provide both quantitative and qualitative behavior-based data (that's the beauty of digital media, isn't it?). I look at metrics such as how many new followers I've gained in the day or who's sharing what. What's even more important is what people post or share (the qualitative side) and the conversation stream that ensues. Once a conversation starts, it shows that people are engaged—once they write something and I respond I become both real and friendly and trustworthy, and people are then more willing to connect with me. There's even a company that makes backpacks that tracks what people are saying on Instagram and forecasts sales based on Instagram comments related to the new backpack designs. That's pretty cool!

For small businesses such as mine, having an analytics plan is really, really important. If you don't want to mess with it or are "too busy," dedicate someone to handle your analytics…someone who knows what's important for your company or organization…they don't have to be a rocket scientist, they just need to understand your business and your KPIs.

CHAPTER 7

Social Media Marketing Best Practices

The following three case studies highlight the social media marketing strategies and tactics of three brands of varying size competing in three unique industries. The first case study features the Old Spice brand and its efforts to grow sales and market share within the men's body wash category. The second involves the surf and skate lifestyle brand Quiksilver Inc. and a social media-fueled global campaign to promote its DC Shoes brand. The third case study features The Roadery, a start-up motorcycle touring company launching its business primarily with social media on a shoestring budget. These three brands are featured in this "Best Practices" chapter because they represent companies of differing size, spending power, and brand stories, yet with common objectives related to their use of social media as a marketing platform.

The Old Spice Guy

This is a shout out to all you metrosexual males—without you groomers and preeners, this case study involving the body wash category would instead have been about some old-school brand attempting to advertise it's old-school men's deodorant in old-school fashion—using paid media such as television to promote some new packaging concept. Yet, in the 1990s and 2000s, men, especially younger ones, began stocking their shower stalls with products other than bars of soap or Pert 2-in-1 shampoo. In the early 2000s, the men's body wash category began to explode, and brands such as Proctor & Gamble's Old Spice, Nivea, and Unilever's Dove and Axe ramped up their product development efforts, advertising spends, and promotional efforts.

The Why

Fast forward to 2009 where the body wash category had been growing year to year by single- and double-digit percentage gains, yet Old Spice's share growth in this market was flat at best. Enter Old Spice's advertising agency Wieden+Kennedy and Isaiah Mustafa, also known as *The Man Your Man Could Smell Like* (MYMCSL). As it developed plans for a February 2010 Super Bowl commercial featuring Mr. Mustafa, the Old Spice guy, Wieden+Kennedy came across an important insight to buying behavior in the men's body wash category—that women influenced or were responsible for over half of all purchases in the category. Prior to the efforts of Axe, Dove, Gillette, Nivea, and Old Spice, women simply bought women's body wash for their boyfriends or husbands. Yet, as the Old Spice guy proclaimed, "Anything is possible when your man smells like Old Spice and not a lady." Hence, the MYMCSL story and campaign was born.

Engagement Objectives

The idea behind the MYMCSL campaign was to do something different from the typical approach to selling men's body wash and to do it with humor and attention-grabbing content; in other words, to develop content that would actually be interesting and engaging. As the Old Spice brand manager noted, "It's always our goal to engage our consumers in a way that's not only entertaining but also relevant, humorous in our own Old Spice tone and worthy of their attention. Digital is perfect because you can quickly gauge the reaction as people are very open to providing feedback to the advertising."[1]

The Story

The story behind the MYMCSL campaign was a humorous narrative depicting the Old Spice guy in a series of over-the-top manly settings. As was the case with past serial-type campaigns (e.g., Bud Light's *Real Men of Genius*), the brilliance of the Old Spice story and ongoing narrative was that it could be repurposed in many different ways or scenes, yet at the same time retaining its native storyline.

The Content (Part One)

The content strategy for MYMCSL was to appeal to both men and women (remember the insight about women's direct and indirect influence on the body wash purchase decision). And because humor appeals universally across sex and across culture, Wieden+Kennedy developed a campaign featuring scenes of the Old Spice guy riding a horse (shirtless, of course), sawing a table (shirtless, of course), and diving off a cliff (you got it, shirtless).[2]

The Initial Distribution Strategy

The fire starter for the MYMCSL campaign actually took place prior to the campaign airing during the 2010 Super Bowl weekend; it went live online several days before the big game. So, owned media (oldspice.com) and online distribution worked together to create awareness and interest in the campaign even before it appeared on national TV (paid media). The combination of online and paid media (TV) thus helped to get people and the press talking about the campaign to the extent that, according to Wieden+Kennedy, Old Spice occupied a 75 percent share of conversation content in the body wash category.

The Content (Part Two)

The MYMCSL campaign didn't end with the initial content created for and around the 2010 Super Bowl. Months after the initial content was distributed via online and broadcast media, Wieden+Kennedy then took the campaign directly to social media and heightened brand engagement for Old Spice through what it calls the *Response* campaign. For three days in July 2010, the Wieden+Kennedy team created and filmed 186 personalized video responses culled from consumers' and celebrities' questions taken from online social platforms like Reddit, Twitter, and Facebook. After filming and editing the short video responses, all 186 responses were posted on YouTube.

KPIs and Analytics

Hence, the Response campaign was born. You can bet that KPIs for the two-part Old Spice campaign that began in February and concluded in

July 2010 included metrics such as sales and category share numbers. Yet Wieden+Kennedy and Old Spice captured numerous other online and social metrics such as overall media impressions, volume of views of the Response campaign videos, overall video views on Old Spice's YouTube Channel, oldspice.com website traffic, as well as Facebook and Twitter activity.

Postcampaign online and social metrics included the following:

- In the week after the Response campaign was launched, there were 34 million views of the Response videos and over 38,000 related YouTube comments, combined with 29 million online views of the 4 original spots created for broadcast media in February 2010.
- Total media impressions reached 1.4 billion 6 months after the initial February campaign.
- In July 2010, the Old Spice YouTube channel had amassed 94 million video views and 122,000 subscribers, making it the number one most viewed sponsored YouTube channel.
- Old Spice's Twitter following increased 2,700 percent to 83,000 followers, and its Facebook fan base increased 800 percent during and after the campaign.
- Traffic at oldspice.com went up 300 percent.

Yet what about bottom-line sales and category share? This is where it gets interesting. It's not difficult to uncover reports of sales lifts as a result of the overall Old Spice MYMCSL campaign pointing to a 106 percent sales gain for Old Spice from the prior year. Although we *are* writing a book on the application of and strategy behind leveraging social media in branding and advertising, it's also important not to look past the inherent challenge of attributing online and social metrics to higher level KPIs such as sales and share gains. To present the MYMCSL campaign metrics accurately, it's important to differentiate cause and effect with correlation.

Without getting too technical, yes, according to industry reports, Old Spice did see a sales lift (106 percent) and gain in market share (4.8 share points). Yet it's important to consider the other factors that might have played a part in the sales rise. For instance, the shopper research firm IRI reports that 2010 was a year defined by heavy couponing and advertising in the body wash category by competitors such as Gillette. It's interesting to note that Gillette's sales, albeit the smallest player in the men's body wash category at the time, were also up 277 percent during the same time period.

The point is that we can and should attribute some (or a lot) of Old Spice's success to Wieden+Kennedy and the Old Spice guy, yet it's difficult to specify exactly how much of it came from the campaign and how much came from promotional offers. The net takeaway from all of this? It's safe to say that the MYMCSL campaign was a success in a number of ways, including significantly raising Old Spice's share of social presence and the positive sentiment it produced, and helping the brand to sell more body wash. Another lesson learned comes from Wieden+Kennedy's creative director on the campaign, who stated that "the biggest thing we learned overall was the importance of keeping your creative ideas [your story] simple...don't overcomplicate things."[3]

DC Shoes

Surfing, paddling, skating, snowboarding, and looking good and feeling good while doing it—that's the Quiksilver Inc. brand promise. The Quiksilver family of brands is made up of surf-inspired products and apparel for men (Quiksilver) and women (Roxy) and skateboarding shoes and apparel (DC Shoes). This case study is centered on a DC Shoes social media campaign developed to promote its skate shoes in 24 cities around the globe.

The Why

The *why* behind the DC Shoes' Go Skateboarding Day celebration and campaign was to promote the idea that the skateboarding culture and lifestyle spans the globe, no matter where you live, whether it's in Barcelona or Shanghai or Los Angeles.

Engagement Objective

Quiksilver Inc. had been losing money for six consecutive years prior to 2013. The reason? The teens and twentysomethings that make up

Quiksilver's core market are a fickle bunch, and teen influence is what drives sales in the surf and skate industry. One year it's Quiksilver, the next year it's Billabong or Rip Curl, and they all compete for share in the *über*competitive surf and skate lifestyle market. In 2013, Quiksilver's new management team began shedding various subbrands to renew its focus on its three flagship brands: Quiksilver, Roxy, and DC Shoes.

Hence, the engagement objective behind DC Shoes' Go Skateboarding Day campaign was to tap into the power of the social media ecosystem and to connect with and activate avid skateboarders in 24 cities around the globe on a treasure hunt for special DC Signature shoes and gift cards.

The Story

The story behind the DC Shoes campaign is one of establishing authenticity and relevance in the highly competitive skate market. After all, what better day to celebrate the DC Shoes brand and its rich history designing skateboarding shoes and apparel than on Go Skateboarding Day? Did you even know such a day existed? So, in June 2013, DC Shoes launched what it called its first ever *Global Digital Product Toss*. It actually hid special DC shoes (yes, real, physical shoes) at popular skate spots and specialty skate stores in 24 major cities, including New York City, Sydney, Toronto, Beijing, Los Angeles, Shanghai, Barcelona, and Tokyo.

The Content

Details on the hidden shoe locations in the 24 cities were revealed every hour, starting with the time zones in the Asia-Pacific region and ending with reveals in California, Quiksilver Inc.'s home base. The campaign headline was *Finders, Keepers. You Find It, It's Yours!*

The calls to action were communicated across the campaign's social media ecosystem, including the DC Shoes website as well as its Facebook and Instagram pages and Twitter. For example, the first reveal took place in Sydney on Day 1[4]:

Stop 1: Sydney, Australia

It's officially Go Skateboarding Day in Australia and the DC Global Product Toss begins! We're stashing DC signature shoes in 24 cities across the globe, kicking it off with this pair of Nyjah Huston signature shoes at this spot next to the Sydney Harbor Bridge. If you're in Sydney, go grab these Nyjahs now, before someone else does!

The Distribution Strategy

The distribution strategy for the Go Skateboarding Day campaign was relatively simple: Enable avid skaters to connect with DC Shoes and participate in the treasure hunt campaign across owned media (the DC Shoes website and its Facebook, Instagram, and Twitter platforms) for clues to shoe and gift card locations.

KPIs and Analytics

Through the Go Skateboarding Day campaign, DC Shoes sought to drive traffic to its website and increase engagement and activity across its social channels of Facebook, Instagram, and Twitter over the 24 hours of the campaign. The campaign results were promising—website activity at dcshoes.com rose significantly during the 24-hour period, and through 60 Facebook posts, the brand generated a total reach of 3.7 million unique individuals along with 7 million social media impressions.

In a more general context, DC Shoes' Go Skateboarding Day/Global Digital Product Toss campaign illustrates how physical brand activity (real products hidden in real locations) was able to drive online social activity, and in turn how online and social media also serve to activate brands' physical presence, including retail involvement and support.

The Roadery

The Roadery's founder, Philipp Reker, developed an interest in and fascination with performance cars and motorcycles long before he relocated from Germany to California. After his university studies, Reker spent several years as a brand manager at Mercedes-Benz in Stuttgart. Yet, an even more interesting opportunity than working for one of the world's leading luxury car brands arose in Southern California, and he subsequently moved to Los Angeles to head entertainment marketing for the advertising agency DDB, working exclusively with the car brand Volkswagen (VW). It was in California that Reker discovered the appeal of the American open road and the beauty that defines much of California's coastline and interior. Leaving DDB to start something new, Reker founded The Roadery, a custom motorcycle touring company (see roadery.com as featured in "The Insider's Perspective" in Chapter 3), in Venice, California, in 2012.

The Why

We work, we live, we struggle to make ends meet—and the inertia sets in. We fall into our daily routines and it becomes hard to escape the demands of our jobs, the multiple screens, the new mortgage, the tough boss. The *why* behind The Roadery is to fight against these forces and to get people out of their routines and out from behind their desks and out onto the open road. Going beyond the standard, cookie-cutter motorcycle tour, Reker founded The Roadery to provide not just an escape (powered by *really cool* bikes) but also a unique, personal, and unforgettable experience to help people reconnect with friends and nature, complete with denim and vintage America.

Engagement Objective

Reker and his team's engagement objective was quite simple: to seduce individuals with compelling and sensual visual content that would help them to experience vicariously what it was like to take part in a Roadery tour. Through the visual content, Reker wanted people to engage in The Roadery experience, in effect taking them on a virtual tour, on a journey, and enabling them to internalize the experience.

The Story

The story behind The Roadery is quite simple and timeless. Remember back in Chapter 3 how we talked about the role of the hero (e.g., Nike) and the outlaw (e.g., Harley-Davidson) in story telling? The Roadery experience is both—the hero, in terms of rescuing people from the mundane and helping them reconnect with friends and the outdoors, and the outlaw in the spirit of the Wild West and offering people a different way to explore Americana on retro motorcycles. Just as with the hero's journey from Chapter 3, The Roadery aims to provide a visually compelling bonding experience with friends old and new—one that helps them be part of a unique adventure in the face of life's headwinds and obstacles (i.e., that pesky mortgage or that demanding job). The following quote posted on lodownmaga-zine.com's blog in an article about The Roadery sums it up well: "The world is in such a rush all the time that we don't get a chance to just be. Years later this leaves us wondering where all the time went and we are sorry that it's all gone."

The Content

Because The Roadery brand was launched with a small advertising and production budget, its content strategy needed to be tightly focused and it had to, as pointed out by Reker, "do a few things really well." First and foremost, the content created for the launch of The Roadery had to some-how capture and convey the experience and excitement of a Roadery tour. Reker decided that video was the best format, and thus a large share of the content production budget went to producing a high-quality launch video and content featuring the elements of the tour that stood out from others, including the landscape, the camaraderie, and of course the bikes themselves.[5]

In short, The Roadery's launch video and its content served as an online and social fire starter. Reker and his team also captured still images to keep the fire going and to perpetuate The Roadery's unique story. Because the video content and photography was of such high quality, Reker also bucked conventional wisdom and determined that user-gen-erated video and photo content from The Roadery tour participants (a potentially helpful strategy) risked failing his stringent quality test. Plus, he did not have the personnel or resources as a start-up venture to prop-erly curate or edit any customer-generated material. Thus, The Roadery's content was homegrown and focused on communicating the experience through compelling video and visuals.

The Distribution Strategy

The unique thing about The Roadery compared with the other two brands in this chapter—Old Spice and Quiksilver—is that its online and social media efforts, as with many start-ups, were initially so prominent in launching the brand and revealing it for the first time to the public. The Roadery's distribution strategy at its beginning parallels a broadcast model, where The Roadery website and its strategic social media platforms were initially a one-way street, communicating its story through the launch video and visuals. In fact, traditional paid media wasn't even part of the equation for the brand. Rather, its content and distribution strategy was based on developing owned media through its website and launch video.

The Roadery's distribution strategy was then dedicated to fostering earned media through its primary social platforms such as Facebook (currently 6,000+ fans), Instagram (currently almost 8,000 followers), Vimeo (with over 30,000 cumulative video views), and a branded YouTube channel where its launch video has been viewed almost 3,000 times. Yet, the important question here is why the focus on Facebook, Instagram, Vimeo, and YouTube? It all goes back to The Roadery story—with Vimeo and YouTube as its primary video distribution channels, Facebook as the all-purpose platform for distributing written and visual content and for enabling comments, testimonials, and sharing, and Instagram as the platform for distributing easily accessed and bite-sized pictorial content.

KPIs and Analytics

The myth of social media marketing, perhaps propagated by high-priced consultants and so-called experts, is that the process of applying analytics has to be complex. With a lean staff, Reker simplified the analytics process so that his team focused on a select few KPIs such as audience relevance and engagement.

For instance, through Facebook and Instagram likes, comments, and shares, and YouTube and Vimeo viewing statistics from analytics platforms such as YouTube Analytics (YTA),[6] Reker assessed the relevance and impact of The Roadery's message and story to its social audience. Using Facebook Insights and Statigram for Instagram metrics, Reker's team monitored the performance of posts and pictures and other content daily to determine what worked and what did not, in an iterative and ongoing experiment of sorts. The result is an analytics plan focused on a few select KPIs and one that taps into some powerful, and free, analytics platforms.

CHAPTER 8

The New Front Line

We all know the numbers to date: 1.2 billion people worldwide on Facebook; almost 200 million Twitter and over 70 million Pinterest users (80 percent women, by the way); 100 hours of video uploaded to YouTube every minute; and 500 years of YouTube videos watched on Facebook every day—this mind-blowing list of social media's reach and its status as the fastest growing medium for content creation goes on and on. As recent as 10 years ago, the volume of content produced and the number of consumer touch points and metrics were nowhere as numerous as they are today. More than that, brands didn't even *need* to consider this complex and still-growing media ecosystem. Life was simple.

Now, every minute of every day we are exposed to and interact with branded content. Think about, from the time you wake up and check your phone for e-mail, LinkedIn, Twitter, or Facebook updates, how omnipresent and ubiquitous branded content has become. What's the first thing you do when your plane lands and taxis to its gate? Many of you pull out your phone and check your e-mail and your Facebook. And your friends and colleagues are doing the same—tweeting and posting and updating and rating and liking and sharing. At the same time, brands are also responding and interacting along with your posting and tweeting. It's an endless cycle of social promotion, conversation, and discussion.

This is the new frontier and what we call *the new front line*. And this is where you and your marketing team need to be. This is also where your other employees need to be, even though they may not be designated to be on the new front line. Welcome to the new world of marketing, branding, and advertising!

As the legendary salesperson and motivational speaker Zig Ziglar once said, "Everybody in a business is capable of breaking a sale." Kind of a downer, huh? Well, it's reality. A perfect example is what happened with

Applebee's in January 2013. A waitress thought she was being funny by posting a picture of a receipt with the customer's signature. It turned into a social media nightmare that in the end cost the waitress her job. A similar thing happened with the 2009 Domino's Pizza franchise video that went viral and landed the two employees in big trouble. They all thought it was funny. Who's laughing now?

Here is what the Applebee's waitress had to say, "When I posted this, I didn't represent Applebee's in a bad light." She continues, "In fact, I didn't represent them at all. I did my best to protect the identity of all parties involved. I didn't break any specific guidelines in the company handbook—I checked." We can almost guarantee that the waitress didn't look at the Applebee's social media policy because as a waitress, why would she have access to it. Too often, if your company does have a social media policy, it's not communicated in the official employee handbook.

The poor waitress was expected to be on the old, not the new, front line. We're pretty sure there is some type of clause in Applebee's social media policy about protecting the brand and acting with integrity. It just didn't reach, curiously, the employees with the most direct impact on and proximity to the customer.

One of the coauthors has had the opportunity to write and read hundreds of social media policies. By far, one of our favorites is that of the *Los Angeles Times*. It talks about and stresses the idea of integrity within the first sentence. It's the first bullet point under the heading "Basic Principles": "Integrity is our most important commodity: Avoid writing or posting anything that would embarrass The Times or compromise your ability to do your job."[1]

That's about as clear as you can get. Then *The Times* goes on to write a simple sentence that is nothing short of brilliant: "Assume that your professional life and your personal life will merge online regardless of your care in separating them."[2]

And right there, dear reader, is the perfect definition of the new front line. Our lives have become blurred; we live in this fuzzy zone that oscillates between the virtual and the physical, between digital and analog. We have jobs and we have our personal lives, and the chances are that we're going to talk about them both and share them online. And that in a nutshell is a brand's biggest nightmare.

to figure out your brand's story and how it can be best told using social media and (2) we want to stress how important it is to communicate *how* you are telling your story through social media, as well as your metrics and results, internally to your bosses and colleagues as well as to other key external stakeholders.

If there is one thing we want you to take away from this book, it is that jumping into a social media strategy without significant thought and reflection is not a good first step. If you start with the *how* and the *what* before you identify your *why, who,* and *what,* there is a good chance you are going to fail. As Peter Drucker, the self-described social ecologist once said, "Unless commitment is made, there are only promises and hopes...but no plans." So think of this book as the first step of many in your commitment to create a long-term social media strategy that will not only inform and inspire your customers, but also engage them for years to come.

The Insider's Perspective

David Knies, chief strategy officer, Breakaway Innovation Group

Branding and marketing can be complex but its goal is simple—connect with people and turn them into customers. Smart marketers focus obsessively on mastering the art of the connection. Social media gives every person and every business new superpowers to connect—even the smallest voice can be a media company today. In an era where everyone is always on—connected via smartphone, tablet, or other devices—people learn about new companies, brands, and campaigns through word-of-mouth and word-of-mouse, and not through traditional advertising. Think about it...when was the last time you heard about something for the first time through a TV spot or print ad? It's now an imperative for a brand to have a social media presence on par with its products and services—in fact, social media is often the first point of connection a person will have with a brand. And, remember that the connection goes both ways. Social media empowers people (your customers) to share and broadcast their thoughts about your brand to their loyal network of followers. Remember when Delta

Airlines charged U.S. military troops returning from Desert Storm for excess baggage? The social media storm did more damage to its brand than all of the advertising they could run, all the stadiums they could put their name on, and all the press releases they could issue. In the words of Doc Searls, coauthor of *The Cluetrain Manifesto,* "Markets are conversations, and conversation is fire; therefore, marketing is arson… you only need one match to start a fire." And, social media is the smart marketer's book of matches.

Notes

Preface

1. Helft (2012).
2. Kotkin (2010).
3. Bedbury (2002).

Chapter 1

1. Hanna, Rohm, and Crittenden (2011).
2. Sinek (2009).
3. Bedbury (2002).
4. Fortini-Campbell (2001).
5. Bedbury (2002).
6. American Marketing Association (2013).
7. simplypsychology.org (n.d.).
8. Schultz and Peltier (2013).

Chapter 2

1. Jacobellis v. Ohio (1964).
2. Donkers et al. (2010) and van Doorn et al. (2010).
3. Rohm, Kaltcheva, and Milne (2013).
4. Kohler, Rohm, de Ruyter, and Wetzels (2011).
5. Graeber and Dolan (2007).

Chapter 3

1. Rutledge (2011).
2. Mycoskie (2011).
3. Fortini-Campbell (2001).
4. Conrad (2010).
5. Rose and Pulizzi (2011).
6. Pulizzi (2012a).
7. Nesterenko (2013).
8. Klara (2011).
9. Howard (2003).

Chapter 4

1. Rose (2013).
2. Lidsky (2011).
3. Pulizzi (2012b).

Chapter 5

1. Pulizzi (2014).

Chapter 6

1. Hemann and Burbary (2013).
2. Krajicek (2013).
3. Wyner (2013).
4. Petouhoff (2012).
5. Zocalogroup (n.d.).

Chapter 7

1. Dandad.org (2013).
2. Old Spice YouTube channel (n.d.).
3. Dandad.org (2013).
4. DCShoes (2013).
5. *The Roadery* (n.d.).
6. YouTube (n.d.).

Chapter 8

1. *Los Angeles Times* (n.d.).
2. *Los Angeles Times* (n.d.).
3. French, LaBerge, and Magill (2011).

References

American Marketing Association. *Definition of Marketing,* 2013, http://www.
marketingpower.com/aboutama/pages/definitionofmarketing.aspx, (accessed
November 15).

Bedbury, S. *A New Brand World.* New York, NY: Penguin Books, 2002.

Conrad, A. *How Hamsters Became Kia's Killer Salesmen,* 2010, http://www.money.
cnn.com/2010/07/02/news/companies/kia_hamsters_advertising.fortune/,
(accessed October 31).

Dandad.org. *Old Spice Response Campaign.* 2013, dandad.org/en/old-spice-
response-campaign, (accessed October 13).

DCShoes. *Stop 1: Sydney, Australia,* 2013, blog.dcshoes.com/us/en/skate/news/
go-skateboarding-day-global-product-toss-06132013?camp=dc_116574,
(accessed November 15).

Donkers, B.; R. Venkatesan; T. Wiesel; and S. Tillmanns. "Undervalued or
Overvalued Customers: Capturing Total Customer Engagement Value."
Journal of Service Research 13, no. 3 (August 2010), pp. 297–310.

Fortini-Campbell, L. *Hitting the Sweet Spot.* Chicago, IL: The Copy Workshop,
2001.

French, T.; L. LaBerge; and P. Magill. *We're All Marketers Now,* 2011, http://www.
mckinsey.com/insights/marketing_sales/were_all_marketers_now, (October
13, 2013).

Graeber, C.; and E. Dolan. "Meet Your Next Financial Customer." *Forrester
Research Report,* March 23, 2007.

Hanna, R.; A. Rohm; and V.L. Crittenden. "We're All Connected: The Power of
the Social Media Ecosystem." *Business Horizons* 54, no. 3 (May–June 2011),
pp. 265–273.

Helft, M. *Pop Went the Social Media Bubble…Now What?,* 2012, http://tech
.fortune.cnn.com/2012/08/16/pop-went-the-social-media-bubble-now-
what/, (accessed September 24, 2013).

Hemann, C.; and K. Burbary. *Digital Marketing Analytics.* Indianapolis, IN: Que
Publishing, 2013.

Howard, T. *Dude! You've Been Replaced,* 2003, http://usatoday30.usato
day.com/money/advertising/adtrack/2003-03-09-adtrack_x.htm, (accessed
November 1, 2013).

Jacobellis v. Ohio, 378 U.S. 184, 197 (1964).

Klara, R. *Insurance: Progressive CMO Jeff Charney,* 2011, http://www.adweek.com/
news/advertising-branding/insurance-progressive-cmo-jeff-charney-135978,
(accessed December 1, 2013).

Kohler, C.; A.J. Rohm; K. de Ruyter; and M.G.M. Wetzels. "Return on Interactivity: The Impact of Online Agents on Newcomer Adjustment." *Journal of Marketing* 75, no. 2 (March 2011), pp. 93–108.

Kotkin, J. *The Changing Demographics of America*, 2010, http://www.smithsonianmag.com/40th-anniversary/the-changing-demographics-of-america-538284/, (accessed December 1, 2013).

Krajicek, D. The ROI of Everything. *Marketing Insights*. Summer, p. 8, 2013.

LA Times Social Media Policy, 2009, http://latimesblogs.latimes.com/readers/2009/11/updated-social-media-guidelines.html, (accessed December 15, 2013).

Lidsky, D. *Storytelling Your Way to Success*, 2011, http://www.fastcompany.com/1734124/storytelling-your-way-success, (accessed November 13, 2013).

Mycoskie, B. *Start Something That Matters*. New York, NY: Spiegel & Grau trade paperbacks, 2011.

Nesterenko, H. *7 Ways to Integrate More Brand Storytelling in Your Content Marketing Strategy*, 2013, http://socialmediatoday.com, (accessed October 13, 2013).

Old Spice YouTube Channel, n.d., http://www.youtube.com/user/OldSpice, (accessed October 13, 2013).

Petouhoff, N.L. "ROI of Social Media: Myths, Truths and How to Measure." *radian6 Community Ebook*, 2013, www.radian6.com, (accessed November 1, 2013).

Pulizzi, J. "The Business Model of Content Marketing." In *Epic Content Marketing*, p. 27. New York, NY: McGraw-Hill Education, 2014.

Pulizzi, J. *Coca-Cola Bets the Farm on Content Marketing: Content 2020*, 2012a, http://www.contentmarketinginstitute.com/2012/01/coca-cola-content-marketing-20-20/, (accessed November 1, 2013).

Pulizzi. J. *History Content Marketing [Infographic]-Corporate Storytelling is Not New*, 2012b, http://contentmarketinginstitute.com/2012/02/history-content-marketing-infographic/, (accessed November 1, 2013).

The Roadery banner video, 2012, theroadery.com, (accessed December 1, 2013).

Rohm, A.J.; V. Kaltcheva; and G.R. Milne. "A Mixed-Method Approach to Examining Brand-Consumer Interactions Driven By Social Media." *Journal of Research in Interactive Marketing*, 7, no. 4 (January 2013), pp. 295–311.

Rose, R. *The CMO.com Interview: Content Marketing Institute Chief Strategist Robert Rose*, 2013, http://www.cmo.com/content/cmo-com/home/articles/2013/7/22/contentmarketinginstitute_cmocom_interview.html, (accessed November 1, 2013).

Rose, R.; and J. Pulizzi. *Managing Content Marketing*. Cleveland, OH: CMI Books, 2011.

Rutledge, P. *The Psychological Power of Storytelling*, 2011, http://www.psychologytoday.com, (accessed November 13, 2013).

Schultz, D.E.; and Peltier, J. "Social Media's Slippery Slope: Challenges, Opportunities and Future Research Directions." *Journal of Research in Interactive Marketing* 7, no. 2 (May 2013), pp. 86–99.

Simplypsychology.org, n.d., simplypsychology.org/Hierarchyofneeds.jpg, (accessed October 15, 2013).

Sinek, S. *How Great Leaders Inspire Action*, 2009, http://www.ted.com/talks/ simon_sinek_how_great_leaders_inspire_action.html, (accessed November 1, 2013).

van Doorn, J.; K.N. Lemon; V. Mittal; S. Nass; D. Pick; P. Pirner; and P.C. Verhoef. "Customer Engagement Behavior: Theoretical Foundations and Research Directions." *Journal of Service Research* 13, no. 3 (August 2010), pp. 253–266.

Wyner, G. Linked In. *Marketing Insights*. Summer, p. 10, 2013.

YouTube, *YouTube Analytics*, n.d., Youtube.com/yt/playbook/yt-analytics.html, (accessed December 15, 2013).

Zocalogroup, n.d., zocalogroup.com/, (accessed December 15, 2013).

Index

DIGITAL AND SOCIAL MEDIA MARKETING AND ADVERTISING COLLECTION HAS MANY FORTHCOMING TITLES, INCLUDING...

Vicky Crittenden, Babson College, Editor

- *Digital and Social Media Marketing: Keeping it Real* by Nathalie Collins
- *Online Consumer Insight* by Geraldine Rosa Henderson
- *Corporate Branding in Facebook Fan Pages: Ideas for Improving Your Brand Value* by Eliane Pereira Zamath Brito
- *Social Media Roots: The First Decade of the Digital Media Leadership in the Influence Economy* by Cindy Gordon
- *Mobile Marketing: A Plan For Strategic Success* by J. Barry Dickinson
- *Mobile Marketing Strategies:* by Karen Mishra
- *Information Privacy in the Marketplace Perspectives on the Information Exchange Between Consumers and Marketers* by George Milne
- *Digital Consumption and Fantasy Football: Lessons For Marketers From America's 'Virtual' Pass Time* by Mujde Yuksel
- *Mobile Commerce: How It Contrasts, Challenges and Enhances Electronic Commerce* by Esther Swilley
- *Electronic Word of Mouth for Service Businesses* by Linda W. Lee
- *Digital Marketing Management: A Handbook for the Current (or Future) CEO* by Debra Zahay
- *Mobile Advertising: Moving from SMS to Mobile Applications* by Aikaterini C. Valvi
- *Presentation Evaluation: How to Inspire, Educate, and Entertain Your Audience* by Michael Weiss
- *M-Powering Marketing in a Mobile World* by Syagnik Banerjee
- *Using and Managing Online Communities* by Edward Boon
- *Viral Marketing and Social Networks* by Maria Petrescu

Announcing the Business Expert Press Digital Library

Concise E-books Business Students Need for Classroom and Research

This book can also be purchased in an e-book collection by your library as
- a one-time purchase,
- that is owned forever,
- allows for simultaneous readers,
- has no restrictions on printing, and
- can be downloaded as PDFs from within the library community.

Our digital library collections are a great solution to beat the rising cost of textbooks. E-books can be loaded into their course management systems or onto students' e-book readers.

The **Business Expert Press** digital libraries are very affordable, with no obligation to buy in future years. For more information, please visit **www.businessexpertpress.com/librarians**. To set up a trial in the United States, please email **sales@businessexpertpress.com**.

DATE DUE	RETURNED
SEP 2 9 2015	OCT 2 2 2015
9/12/17	

CPSIA information can be obtained at www.ICGtesting.com
Printed in the USA
LVOW10s2138121214

418641LV00010B/163/P

9 781606 498385